C-3314   CAREER EXAMINATION SERIES

This is your
PASSBOOK for...

Window Clerk (USPS)

Test Preparation Study Guide
Questions & Answers

COPYRIGHT NOTICE

This book is SOLELY intended for, is sold ONLY to, and its use is RESTRICTED to individual, bona fide applicants or candidates who qualify by virtue of having seriously filed applications for appropriate license, certificate, professional and/or promotional advancement, higher school matriculation, scholarship, or other legitimate requirements of education and/or governmental authorities.

This book is NOT intended for use, class instruction, tutoring, training, duplication, copying, reprinting, excerption, or adaptation, etc., by:

1) Other publishers
2) Proprietors and/or Instructors of "Coaching" and/or Preparatory Courses
3) Personnel and/or Training Divisions of commercial, industrial, and governmental organizations
4) Schools, colleges, or universities and/or their departments and staffs, including teachers and other personnel
5) Testing Agencies or Bureaus
6) Study groups which seek by the purchase of a single volume to copy and/or duplicate and/or adapt this material for use by the group as a whole without having purchased individual volumes for each of the members of the group
7) Et al.

Such persons would be in violation of appropriate Federal and State statutes.

PROVISION OF LICENSING AGREEMENTS – Recognized educational, commercial, industrial, and governmental institutions and organizations, and others legitimately engaged in educational pursuits, including training, testing, and measurement activities, may address request for a licensing agreement to the copyright owners, who will determine whether, and under what conditions, including fees and charges, the materials in this book may be used them. In other words, a licensing facility exists for the legitimate use of the material in this book on other than an individual basis. However, it is asseverated and affirmed here that the material in this book CANNOT be used without the receipt of the express permission of such a licensing agreement from the Publishers. Inquiries re licensing should be addressed to the company, attention rights and permissions department.

All rights reserved, including the right of reproduction in whole or in part, in any form or by any means, electronic or mechanical, including photocopying, recording, or by any information storage and retrieval system, without permission in writing from the Publisher.

Copyright © 2024 by
National Learning Corporation

212 Michael Drive, Syosset, NY 11791
(516) 921-8888 • www.passbooks.com
E-mail: info@passbooks.com

PUBLISHED IN THE UNITED STATES OF AMERICA

PASSBOOK® SERIES

THE *PASSBOOK® SERIES* has been created to prepare applicants and candidates for the ultimate academic battlefield – the examination room.

At some time in our lives, each and every one of us may be required to take an examination – for validation, matriculation, admission, qualification, registration, certification, or licensure.

Based on the assumption that every applicant or candidate has met the basic formal educational standards, has taken the required number of courses, and read the necessary texts, the *PASSBOOK® SERIES* furnishes the one special preparation which may assure passing with confidence, instead of failing with insecurity. Examination questions – together with answers – are furnished as the basic vehicle for study so that the mysteries of the examination and its compounding difficulties may be eliminated or diminished by a sure method.

This book is meant to help you pass your examination provided that you qualify and are serious in your objective.

The entire field is reviewed through the huge store of content information which is succinctly presented through a provocative and challenging approach – the question-and-answer method.

A climate of success is established by furnishing the correct answers at the end of each test.

You soon learn to recognize types of questions, forms of questions, and patterns of questioning. You may even begin to anticipate expected outcomes.

You perceive that many questions are repeated or adapted so that you can gain acute insights, which may enable you to score many sure points.

You learn how to confront new questions, or types of questions, and to attack them confidently and work out the correct answers.

You note objectives and emphases, and recognize pitfalls and dangers, so that you may make positive educational adjustments.

Moreover, you are kept fully informed in relation to new concepts, methods, practices, and directions in the field.

You discover that you are actually taking the examination all the time: you are preparing for the examination by "taking" an examination, not by reading extraneous and/or supererogatory textbooks.

In short, this PASSBOOK®, used directedly, should be an important factor in helping you to pass your test.

WINDOW CLERK, USPS

DUTIES
Sells stamps and other postal products to the public, collects postage dues, and performs related duties at retail windows at post offices.

SCOPE OF THE EXAMINATION
The written test is designed to test for knowledge, skills, and/or abilities in such areas as:
1. Classifying mail;
2. Handling postage due, certified and registered mail;
3. Postal forms and their uses;
4. Retailing postal products; and
5. Postal arithmetic.

WHAT IS THIS BOOK ALL ABOUT?

This book will give you a good idea of what you have to do when you take the Civil Service tests for jobs in the Post Office.

- —It shows how to apply for the test.
- —It explains how to do the different kinds of questions.
- —It describes how to mark your answers on the answer sheet.
- —It gives some of each kind of question to try.
- —Finally, it gives you a chance to test yourself with tests just like those used in the examination—same kinds of questions, same difficulty, same length.

The material is arranged so that you can study by yourself. Read the explanation, try the questions, check your answers. For the questions you get wrong, try to figure out why the correct answer is right and why you made a mistake. If you are working by yourself and you can't figure out why the correct answer is right, try to get some help. Ask a teacher; a librarian; perhaps a brother, a sister, or friend who has gone to high school.

SO YOU WANT TO WORK FOR THE POST OFFICE

THAT'S GREAT!

But... Did You Know

- You have to be 18 or over
  (16 if you are a high school graduate)
- You have to pass a physical examination
- You have to be a United States citizen
- YOU HAVE TO PASS A CIVIL SERVICE TEST

You will find in this book   tests that are very much like the tests you have to take to get a job in the Post Office.

READ AND STUDY THIS BOOK   CAREFULLY.

HERE ARE SOME POST OFFICE JOBS

- You could be a MAIL HANDLER.
  You would help move the mail (it's heavy) within the Post Office building.

- You could be a DISTRIBUTION CLERK.
  You would sort the mail (in some places by hand, in some places by machine) and do other things to keep the mail moving

- You could be a MAIL CARRIER.
  You would deliver mail to homes, stores, and offices.

YOU MUST TAKE AND PASS A CIVIL SERVICE TEST IN ORDER TO BE HIRED FOR ANY OF THESE JOBS.

(There are sometimes openings for DRIVERS and GARAGEMEN. There are not many of these jobs, but it's worth checking with your local Post Office or the Federal Job Information Center if you're interested.)

How Do You Apply for a Post Office Job?

FIRST: Go to your nearest Post Office or Federal Job Information Center. Tell them you want to apply for a Post Office job. You will get a form to fill out.

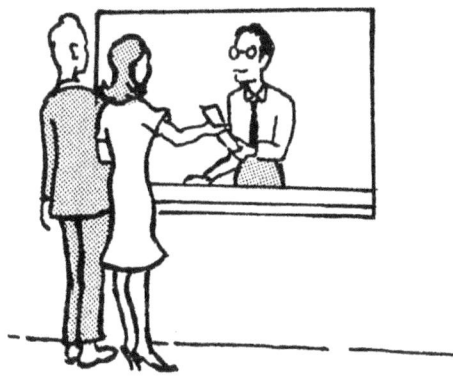

(If they are not accepting applications now, find out when they expect to accept them again. It might be a good idea to start getting ready for the examination anyway.)

You can find the address of your nearest Post Office or Federal Job Information Center in the telephone book.

When you get this form, be sure to find out WHEN you have to send it in, and WHERE you send it.

SECOND: Look over the form. If you don't know how to answer all the questions, ask someone in the office or someone you know for help. If there is no one to help you,

- Answer all the questions the best you can.
- Be sure to print your name and address.

This is what the Application Form looks like

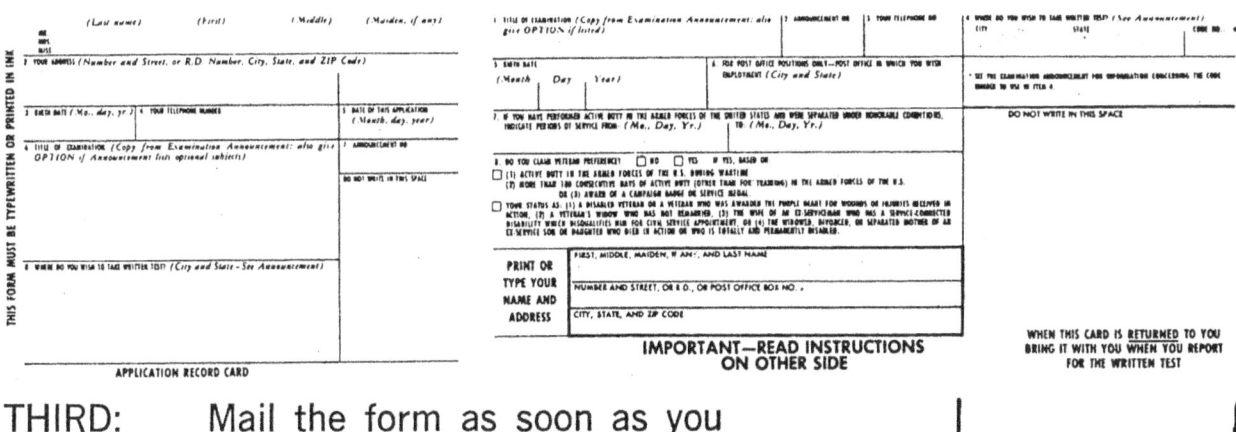

THIRD: Mail the form as soon as you can. (Part of it will be returned to you, telling you when and where to report for the test.)

After You Send in Your Application Form

You have mailed in your application form. Soon, you will get back the part that tells you when and where to take the Civil Service test. This is called your admission card. It looks like this:

1. TITLE OF EXAMINATION (Copy from Examination Announcement; also give OPTION if listed)	2. ANNOUNCEMENT NO.	3. YOUR TELEPHONE NO.	4. WHERE DO YOU WISH TO TAKE WRITTEN TEST? (See Announcement) CITY: STATE: CODE NO.: *
5. BIRTH DATE (Month Day Year)	6. FOR POST OFFICE POSITIONS ONLY—POST OFFICE IN WHICH YOU WISH EMPLOYMENT (City and State)		* SEE THE EXAMINATION ANNOUNCEMENT FOR INFORMATION CONCERNING THE CODE NUMBER TO USE IN ITEM 4.
7. IF YOU HAVE PERFORMED ACTIVE DUTY IN THE ARMED FORCES OF THE UNITED STATES AND WERE SEPARATED UNDER HONORABLE CONDITIONS, INDICATE PERIODS OF SERVICE FROM: (Mo., Day, Yr.) TO: (Mo., Day, Yr.)			DO NOT WRITE IN THIS SPACE
8. DO YOU CLAIM VETERAN PREFERENCE? ☐ NO ☐ YES IF YES, BASED ON: ☐ (1) ACTIVE DUTY IN THE ARMED FORCES OF THE U.S. DURING WARTIME (2) MORE THAN 180 CONSECUTIVE DAYS OF ACTIVE DUTY (OTHER THAN FOR TRAINING) IN THE ARMED FORCES OF THE U.S. OR (3) AWARD OF A CAMPAIGN BADGE OR SERVICE MEDAL. ☐ YOUR STATUS AS: (1) A DISABLED VETERAN OR A VETERAN WHO WAS AWARDED THE PURPLE HEART FOR WOUNDS OR INJURIES RECEIVED IN ACTION, (2) A VETERAN'S WIDOW WHO HAS NOT REMARRIED, (3) THE WIFE OF AN EX-SERVICEMAN WHO HAS A SERVICE-CONNECTED DISABILITY WHICH DISQUALIFIES HIM FOR CIVIL SERVICE APPOINTMENT, OR (4) THE WIDOWED, DIVORCED, OR SEPARATED MOTHER OF AN EX-SERVICE SON OR DAUGHTER WHO DIED IN ACTION OR WHO IS TOTALLY AND PERMANENTLY DISABLED.			You will be told here where and when to report for your test.
PRINT OR TYPE YOUR NAME AND ADDRESS	FIRST, MIDDLE, MAIDEN, IF ANY, AND LAST NAME NUMBER AND STREET, OR R.D., OR POST OFFICE BOX NO. CITY, STATE, AND ZIP CODE		

IMPORTANT—READ INSTRUCTIONS ON OTHER SIDE

WHEN THIS CARD IS <u>RETURNED</u> TO YOU BRING IT WITH YOU WHEN YOU REPORT FOR THE WRITTEN TEST

Of course, if you did not put down your correct address, or if you forgot to put in your name, you will not hear from anybody.

DO IT RIGHT.

... DON'T GET JITTERY JUST BECAUSE
YOU HAVE TO TAKE A TEST.

Go over the tests in this book   as carefully as you can.
This will help you get ready to take the real test.

AND REMEMBER WHEN YOU SHOW UP

- Be Sure You Have Had
  A Good Night's Sleep

- Be On Time

- Bring Your Admission Card

IF YOU FORGET TO BRING YOUR ADMISSION CARD, YOU WILL
HAVE TO COME BACK ANOTHER TIME, DON'T FORGET

GOOD LUCK...

HOW TO MARK YOUR ANSWER SHEET

The Answer Sheet is where you mark your answers. Your score on the test depends on the marks you make on your Answer Sheet. Therefore, you must mark it exactly the way you are told in the examination room. Some advice on how to use the Answer Sheet is given on this page.

On the next page, you see what a whole Answer Sheet looks like.

Notice how the numbers on the Answer Sheet run across the page—like this:

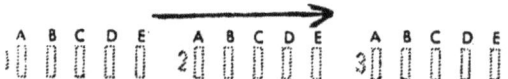

Your answer mark should look LIKE THIS ⟶ ▌
A neat, heavy line, inside the box.

Do NOT mark your answers like this ⟶ ✗ or ⊘ or ∕ or ▆

Don't take a long time to make your marks. Make a heavy pencil mark and move on to the next question.

For practice, mark the boxes for the following number-letter combinations on the Answer Sheet on the next page. The first four in PART A have been done to show how; you do the rest of PART A—

PART A—1A   2A   3D   4A   5D   6A   7D   8A   9A   10D   11D
12A   13A   14A   15D   16D

Now mark the boxes for the following number-letter combinations in PART B.

PART B—1B   2C   3A   4D   5E   6E   7A   8E   9D   10D   11B
12C   13C   14D   15E

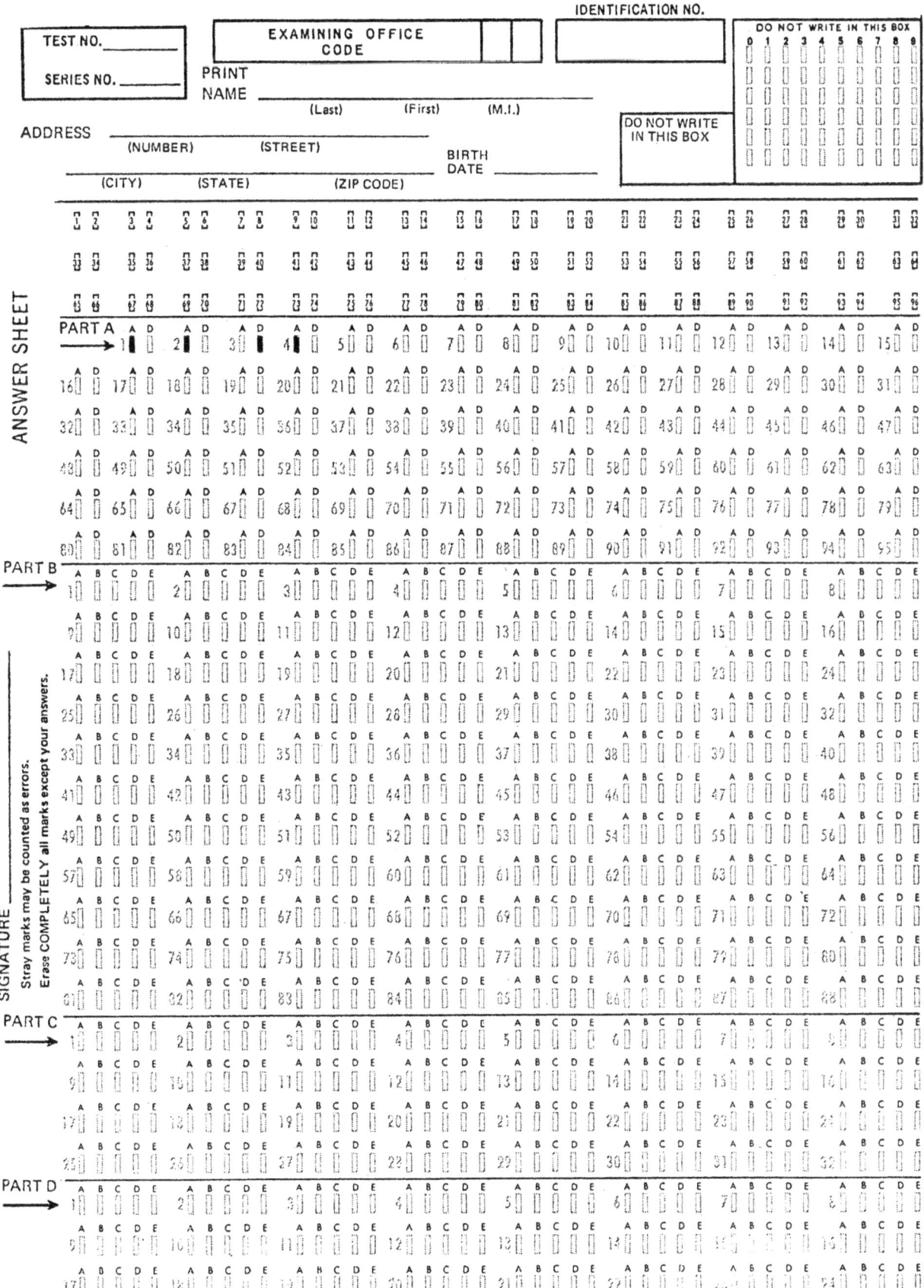

HOW TO TAKE A TEST

I. YOU MUST PASS AN EXAMINATION

A. WHAT EVERY CANDIDATE SHOULD KNOW

Examination applicants often ask us for help in preparing for the written test. What can I study in advance? What kinds of questions will be asked? How will the test be given? How will the papers be graded?

As an applicant for a civil service examination, you may be wondering about some of these things. Our purpose here is to suggest effective methods of advance study and to describe civil service examinations.

Your chances for success on this examination can be increased if you know how to prepare. Those "pre-examination jitters" can be reduced if you know what to expect. You can even experience an adventure in good citizenship if you know why civil service exams are given.

B. WHY ARE CIVIL SERVICE EXAMINATIONS GIVEN?

Civil service examinations are important to you in two ways. As a citizen, you want public jobs filled by employees who know how to do their work. As a job seeker, you want a fair chance to compete for that job on an equal footing with other candidates. The best-known means of accomplishing this two-fold goal is the competitive examination.

Exams are widely publicized throughout the nation. They may be administered for jobs in federal, state, city, municipal, town or village governments or agencies.

Any citizen may apply, with some limitations, such as the age or residence of applicants. Your experience and education may be reviewed to see whether you meet the requirements for the particular examination. When these requirements exist, they are reasonable and applied consistently to all applicants. Thus, a competitive examination may cause you some uneasiness now, but it is your privilege and safeguard.

C. HOW ARE CIVIL SERVICE EXAMS DEVELOPED?

Examinations are carefully written by trained technicians who are specialists in the field known as "psychological measurement," in consultation with recognized authorities in the field of work that the test will cover. These experts recommend the subject matter areas or skills to be tested; only those knowledges or skills important to your success on the job are included. The most reliable books and source materials available are used as references. Together, the experts and technicians judge the difficulty level of the questions.

Test technicians know how to phrase questions so that the problem is clearly stated. Their ethics do not permit "trick" or "catch" questions. Questions may have been tried out on sample groups, or subjected to statistical analysis, to determine their usefulness.

Written tests are often used in combination with performance tests, ratings of training and experience, and oral interviews. All of these measures combine to form the best-known means of finding the right person for the right job.

II. HOW TO PASS THE WRITTEN TEST

A. NATURE OF THE EXAMINATION

To prepare intelligently for civil service examinations, you should know how they differ from school examinations you have taken. In school you were assigned certain definite pages to read or subjects to cover. The examination questions were quite detailed and usually emphasized memory. Civil service exams, on the other hand, try to discover your present ability to perform the duties of a position, plus your potentiality to learn these duties. In other words, a civil service exam attempts to predict how successful you will be. Questions cover such a broad area that they cannot be as minute and detailed as school exam questions.

In the public service similar kinds of work, or positions, are grouped together in one "class." This process is known as *position-classification*. All the positions in a class are paid according to the salary range for that class. One class title covers all of these positions, and they are all tested by the same examination.

B. FOUR BASIC STEPS

1) Study the announcement

How, then, can you know what subjects to study? Our best answer is: "Learn as much as possible about the class of positions for which you've applied." The exam will test the knowledge, skills and abilities needed to do the work.

Your most valuable source of information about the position you want is the official exam announcement. This announcement lists the training and experience qualifications. Check these standards and apply only if you come reasonably close to meeting them.

The brief description of the position in the examination announcement offers some clues to the subjects which will be tested. Think about the job itself. Review the duties in your mind. Can you perform them, or are there some in which you are rusty? Fill in the blank spots in your preparation.

Many jurisdictions preview the written test in the exam announcement by including a section called "Knowledge and Abilities Required," "Scope of the Examination," or some similar heading. Here you will find out specifically what fields will be tested.

2) Review your own background

Once you learn in general what the position is all about, and what you need to know to do the work, ask yourself which subjects you already know fairly well and which need improvement. You may wonder whether to concentrate on improving your strong areas or on building some background in your fields of weakness. When the announcement has specified "some knowledge" or "considerable knowledge," or has used adjectives like "beginning principles of…" or "advanced … methods," you can get a clue as to the number and difficulty of questions to be asked in any given field. More questions, and hence broader coverage, would be included for those subjects which are more important in the work. Now weigh your strengths and weaknesses against the job requirements and prepare accordingly.

3) Determine the level of the position

Another way to tell how intensively you should prepare is to understand the level of the job for which you are applying. Is it the entering level? In other words, is this the position in which beginners in a field of work are hired? Or is it an intermediate or advanced level? Sometimes this is indicated by such words as "Junior" or "Senior" in the class title. Other jurisdictions use Roman numerals to designate the level – Clerk I, Clerk II, for example. The word "Supervisor" sometimes appears in the title. If the level is not indicated by the title, check the description of duties. Will you be working under very close supervision, or will you have responsibility for independent decisions in this work?

4) Choose appropriate study materials

Now that you know the subjects to be examined and the relative amount of each subject to be covered, you can choose suitable study materials. For beginning level jobs, or even advanced ones, if you have a pronounced weakness in some aspect of your training, read a modern, standard textbook in that field. Be sure it is up to date and has general coverage. Such books are normally available at your library, and the librarian will be glad to help you locate one. For entry-level positions, questions of appropriate difficulty are chosen – neither highly advanced questions, nor those too simple. Such questions require careful thought but not advanced training.

If the position for which you are applying is technical or advanced, you will read more advanced, specialized material. If you are already familiar with the basic principles of your field, elementary textbooks would waste your time. Concentrate on advanced textbooks and technical periodicals. Think through the concepts and review difficult problems in your field.

These are all general sources. You can get more ideas on your own initiative, following these leads. For example, training manuals and publications of the government agency which employs workers in your field can be useful, particularly for technical and professional positions. A letter or visit to the government department involved may result in more specific study suggestions, and certainly will provide you with a more definite idea of the exact nature of the position you are seeking.

III. KINDS OF TESTS

Tests are used for purposes other than measuring knowledge and ability to perform specified duties. For some positions, it is equally important to test ability to make adjustments to new situations or to profit from training. In others, basic mental abilities not dependent on information are essential. Questions which test these things may not appear as pertinent to the duties of the position as those which test for knowledge and information. Yet they are often highly important parts of a fair examination. For very general questions, it is almost impossible to help you direct your study efforts. What we can do is to point out some of the more common of these general abilities needed in public service positions and describe some typical questions.

1) General information

Broad, general information has been found useful for predicting job success in some kinds of work. This is tested in a variety of ways, from vocabulary lists to questions about current events. Basic background in some field of work, such as sociology or economics, may be sampled in a group of questions. Often these are principles which have become familiar to most persons through exposure rather than through formal training. It is difficult to advise you how to study for these questions; being alert to the world around you is our best suggestion.

2) Verbal ability

An example of an ability needed in many positions is verbal or language ability. Verbal ability is, in brief, the ability to use and understand words. Vocabulary and grammar tests are typical measures of this ability. Reading comprehension or paragraph interpretation questions are common in many kinds of civil service tests. You are given a paragraph of written material and asked to find its central meaning.

3) Numerical ability
Number skills can be tested by the familiar arithmetic problem, by checking paired lists of numbers to see which are alike and which are different, or by interpreting charts and graphs. In the latter test, a graph may be printed in the test booklet which you are asked to use as the basis for answering questions.

4) Observation
A popular test for law-enforcement positions is the observation test. A picture is shown to you for several minutes, then taken away. Questions about the picture test your ability to observe both details and larger elements.

5) Following directions
In many positions in the public service, the employee must be able to carry out written instructions dependably and accurately. You may be given a chart with several columns, each column listing a variety of information. The questions require you to carry out directions involving the information given in the chart.

6) Skills and aptitudes
Performance tests effectively measure some manual skills and aptitudes. When the skill is one in which you are trained, such as typing or shorthand, you can practice. These tests are often very much like those given in business school or high school courses. For many of the other skills and aptitudes, however, no short-time preparation can be made. Skills and abilities natural to you or that you have developed throughout your lifetime are being tested.

Many of the general questions just described provide all the data needed to answer the questions and ask you to use your reasoning ability to find the answers. Your best preparation for these tests, as well as for tests of facts and ideas, is to be at your physical and mental best. You, no doubt, have your own methods of getting into an exam-taking mood and keeping "in shape." The next section lists some ideas on this subject.

IV. KINDS OF QUESTIONS

Only rarely is the "essay" question, which you answer in narrative form, used in civil service tests. Civil service tests are usually of the short-answer type. Full instructions for answering these questions will be given to you at the examination. But in case this is your first experience with short-answer questions and separate answer sheets, here is what you need to know:

1) **Multiple-choice Questions**
Most popular of the short-answer questions is the "multiple choice" or "best answer" question. It can be used, for example, to test for factual knowledge, ability to solve problems or judgment in meeting situations found at work.
A multiple-choice question is normally one of three types—
- It can begin with an incomplete statement followed by several possible endings. You are to find the one ending which *best* completes the statement, although some of the others may not be entirely wrong.
- It can also be a complete statement in the form of a question which is answered by choosing one of the statements listed.

- It can be in the form of a problem – again you select the best answer.

Here is an example of a multiple-choice question with a discussion which should give you some clues as to the method for choosing the right answer:

When an employee has a complaint about his assignment, the action which will *best* help him overcome his difficulty is to
    A. discuss his difficulty with his coworkers
    B. take the problem to the head of the organization
    C. take the problem to the person who gave him the assignment
    D. say nothing to anyone about his complaint

In answering this question, you should study each of the choices to find which is best. Consider choice "A" – Certainly an employee may discuss his complaint with fellow employees, but no change or improvement can result, and the complaint remains unresolved. Choice "B" is a poor choice since the head of the organization probably does not know what assignment you have been given, and taking your problem to him is known as "going over the head" of the supervisor. The supervisor, or person who made the assignment, is the person who can clarify it or correct any injustice. Choice "C" is, therefore, correct. To say nothing, as in choice "D," is unwise. Supervisors have and interest in knowing the problems employees are facing, and the employee is seeking a solution to his problem.

2) True/False Questions

The "true/false" or "right/wrong" form of question is sometimes used. Here a complete statement is given. Your job is to decide whether the statement is right or wrong.

SAMPLE: A roaming cell-phone call to a nearby city costs less than a non-roaming call to a distant city.

This statement is wrong, or false, since roaming calls are more expensive.

This is not a complete list of all possible question forms, although most of the others are variations of these common types. You will always get complete directions for answering questions. Be sure you understand *how* to mark your answers – ask questions until you do.

V. RECORDING YOUR ANSWERS

Computer terminals are used more and more today for many different kinds of exams.
For an examination with very few applicants, you may be told to record your answers in the test booklet itself. Separate answer sheets are much more common. If this separate answer sheet is to be scored by machine – and this is often the case – it is highly important that you mark your answers correctly in order to get credit.
An electronic scoring machine is often used in civil service offices because of the speed with which papers can be scored. Machine-scored answer sheets must be marked with a pencil, which will be given to you. This pencil has a high graphite content which responds to the electronic scoring machine. As a matter of fact, stray dots may register as answers, so do not let your pencil rest on the answer sheet while you are pondering the correct answer. Also, if your pencil lead breaks or is otherwise defective, ask for another.

Since the answer sheet will be dropped in a slot in the scoring machine, be careful not to bend the corners or get the paper crumpled.

The answer sheet normally has five vertical columns of numbers, with 30 numbers to a column. These numbers correspond to the question numbers in your test booklet. After each number, going across the page are four or five pairs of dotted lines. These short dotted lines have small letters or numbers above them. The first two pairs may also have a "T" or "F" above the letters. This indicates that the first two pairs only are to be used if the questions are of the true-false type. If the questions are multiple choice, disregard the "T" and "F" and pay attention only to the small letters or numbers.

Answer your questions in the manner of the sample that follows:

32. The largest city in the United States is
    A. Washington, D.C.
    B. New York City
    C. Chicago
    D. Detroit
    E. San Francisco

1) Choose the answer you think is best. (New York City is the largest, so "B" is correct.)
2) Find the row of dotted lines numbered the same as the question you are answering. (Find row number 32)
3) Find the pair of dotted lines corresponding to the answer. (Find the pair of lines under the mark "B.")
4) Make a solid black mark between the dotted lines.

VI. BEFORE THE TEST

Common sense will help you find procedures to follow to get ready for an examination. Too many of us, however, overlook these sensible measures. Indeed, nervousness and fatigue have been found to be the most serious reasons why applicants fail to do their best on civil service tests. Here is a list of reminders:

- Begin your preparation early – Don't wait until the last minute to go scurrying around for books and materials or to find out what the position is all about.
- Prepare continuously – An hour a night for a week is better than an all-night cram session. This has been definitely established. What is more, a night a week for a month will return better dividends than crowding your study into a shorter period of time.
- Locate the place of the exam – You have been sent a notice telling you when and where to report for the examination. If the location is in a different town or otherwise unfamiliar to you, it would be well to inquire the best route and learn something about the building.
- Relax the night before the test – Allow your mind to rest. Do not study at all that night. Plan some mild recreation or diversion; then go to bed early and get a good night's sleep.
- Get up early enough to make a leisurely trip to the place for the test – This way unforeseen events, traffic snarls, unfamiliar buildings, etc. will not upset you.
- Dress comfortably – A written test is not a fashion show. You will be known by number and not by name, so wear something comfortable.

- Leave excess paraphernalia at home – Shopping bags and odd bundles will get in your way. You need bring only the items mentioned in the official notice you received; usually everything you need is provided. Do not bring reference books to the exam. They will only confuse those last minutes and be taken away from you when in the test room.
- Arrive somewhat ahead of time – If because of transportation schedules you must get there very early, bring a newspaper or magazine to take your mind off yourself while waiting.
- Locate the examination room – When you have found the proper room, you will be directed to the seat or part of the room where you will sit. Sometimes you are given a sheet of instructions to read while you are waiting. Do not fill out any forms until you are told to do so; just read them and be prepared.
- Relax and prepare to listen to the instructions
- If you have any physical problem that may keep you from doing your best, be sure to tell the test administrator. If you are sick or in poor health, you really cannot do your best on the exam. You can come back and take the test some other time.

VII. AT THE TEST

The day of the test is here and you have the test booklet in your hand. The temptation to get going is very strong. Caution! There is more to success than knowing the right answers. You must know how to identify your papers and understand variations in the type of short-answer question used in this particular examination. Follow these suggestions for maximum results from your efforts:

1) Cooperate with the monitor

The test administrator has a duty to create a situation in which you can be as much at ease as possible. He will give instructions, tell you when to begin, check to see that you are marking your answer sheet correctly, and so on. He is not there to guard you, although he will see that your competitors do not take unfair advantage. He wants to help you do your best.

2) Listen to all instructions

Don't jump the gun! Wait until you understand all directions. In most civil service tests you get more time than you need to answer the questions. So don't be in a hurry. Read each word of instructions until you clearly understand the meaning. Study the examples, listen to all announcements and follow directions. Ask questions if you do not understand what to do.

3) Identify your papers

Civil service exams are usually identified by number only. You will be assigned a number; you must not put your name on your test papers. Be sure to copy your number correctly. Since more than one exam may be given, copy your exact examination title.

4) Plan your time

Unless you are told that a test is a "speed" or "rate of work" test, speed itself is usually not important. Time enough to answer all the questions will be provided, but this does not mean that you have all day. An overall time limit has been set. Divide the total time (in minutes) by the number of questions to determine the approximate time you have for each question.

5) Do not linger over difficult questions

If you come across a difficult question, mark it with a paper clip (useful to have along) and come back to it when you have been through the booklet. One caution if you do this – be sure to skip a number on your answer sheet as well. Check often to be sure that you have not lost your place and that you are marking in the row numbered the same as the question you are answering.

6) Read the questions

Be sure you know what the question asks! Many capable people are unsuccessful because they failed to *read* the questions correctly.

7) Answer all questions

Unless you have been instructed that a penalty will be deducted for incorrect answers, it is better to guess than to omit a question.

8) Speed tests

It is often better NOT to guess on speed tests. It has been found that on timed tests people are tempted to spend the last few seconds before time is called in marking answers at random – without even reading them – in the hope of picking up a few extra points. To discourage this practice, the instructions may warn you that your score will be "corrected" for guessing. That is, a penalty will be applied. The incorrect answers will be deducted from the correct ones, or some other penalty formula will be used.

9) Review your answers

If you finish before time is called, go back to the questions you guessed or omitted to give them further thought. Review other answers if you have time.

10) Return your test materials

If you are ready to leave before others have finished or time is called, take ALL your materials to the monitor and leave quietly. Never take any test material with you. The monitor can discover whose papers are not complete, and taking a test booklet may be grounds for disqualification.

VIII. EXAMINATION TECHNIQUES

1) Read the general instructions carefully. These are usually printed on the first page of the exam booklet. As a rule, these instructions refer to the timing of the examination; the fact that you should not start work until the signal and must stop work at a signal, etc. If there are any *special* instructions, such as a choice of questions to be answered, make sure that you note this instruction carefully.

2) When you are ready to start work on the examination, that is as soon as the signal has been given, read the instructions to each question booklet, underline any key words or phrases, such as *least, best, outline, describe* and the like. In this way you will tend to answer as requested rather than discover on reviewing your paper that you *listed without describing*, that you selected the *worst* choice rather than the *best* choice, etc.

3) If the examination is of the objective or multiple-choice type – that is, each question will also give a series of possible answers: A, B, C or D, and you are called upon to select the best answer and write the letter next to that answer on your answer paper – it is advisable to start answering each question in turn. There may be anywhere from 50 to 100 such questions in the three or four hours allotted and you can see how much time would be taken if you read through all the questions before beginning to answer any. Furthermore, if you come across a question or group of questions which you know would be difficult to answer, it would undoubtedly affect your handling of all the other questions.

4) If the examination is of the essay type and contains but a few questions, it is a moot point as to whether you should read all the questions before starting to answer any one. Of course, if you are given a choice – say five out of seven and the like – then it is essential to read all the questions so you can eliminate the two that are most difficult. If, however, you are asked to answer all the questions, there may be danger in trying to answer the easiest one first because you may find that you will spend too much time on it. The best technique is to answer the first question, then proceed to the second, etc.

5) Time your answers. Before the exam begins, write down the time it started, then add the time allowed for the examination and write down the time it must be completed, then divide the time available somewhat as follows:
    - If 3-1/2 hours are allowed, that would be 210 minutes. If you have 80 objective-type questions, that would be an average of 2-1/2 minutes per question. Allow yourself no more than 2 minutes per question, or a total of 160 minutes, which will permit about 50 minutes to review.
    - If for the time allotment of 210 minutes there are 7 essay questions to answer, that would average about 30 minutes a question. Give yourself only 25 minutes per question so that you have about 35 minutes to review.

6) The most important instruction is to *read each question* and make sure you know what is wanted. The second most important instruction is to *time yourself properly* so that you answer every question. The third most important instruction is to *answer every question*. Guess if you have to but include something for each question. Remember that you will receive no credit for a blank and will probably receive some credit if you write something in answer to an essay question. If you guess a letter – say "B" for a multiple-choice question – you may have guessed right. If you leave a blank as an answer to a multiple-choice question, the examiners may respect your feelings but it will not add a point to your score. Some exams may penalize you for wrong answers, so in such cases *only*, you may not want to guess unless you have some basis for your answer.

7) Suggestions
    a. Objective-type questions
        1. Examine the question booklet for proper sequence of pages and questions
        2. Read all instructions carefully
        3. Skip any question which seems too difficult; return to it after all other questions have been answered
        4. Apportion your time properly; do not spend too much time on any single question or group of questions

5. Note and underline key words – *all, most, fewest, least, best, worst, same, opposite,* etc.
6. Pay particular attention to negatives
7. Note unusual option, e.g., unduly long, short, complex, different or similar in content to the body of the question
8. Observe the use of "hedging" words – *probably, may, most likely,* etc.
9. Make sure that your answer is put next to the same number as the question
10. Do not second-guess unless you have good reason to believe the second answer is definitely more correct
11. Cross out original answer if you decide another answer is more accurate; do not erase until you are ready to hand your paper in
12. Answer all questions; guess unless instructed otherwise
13. Leave time for review

  b. Essay questions
1. Read each question carefully
2. Determine exactly what is wanted. Underline key words or phrases.
3. Decide on outline or paragraph answer
4. Include many different points and elements unless asked to develop any one or two points or elements
5. Show impartiality by giving pros and cons unless directed to select one side only
6. Make and write down any assumptions you find necessary to answer the questions
7. Watch your English, grammar, punctuation and choice of words
8. Time your answers; don't crowd material

8) Answering the essay question

Most essay questions can be answered by framing the specific response around several key words or ideas. Here are a few such key words or ideas:

M's: manpower, materials, methods, money, management
P's: purpose, program, policy, plan, procedure, practice, problems, pitfalls, personnel, public relations

  a. Six basic steps in handling problems:
1. Preliminary plan and background development
2. Collect information, data and facts
3. Analyze and interpret information, data and facts
4. Analyze and develop solutions as well as make recommendations
5. Prepare report and sell recommendations
6. Install recommendations and follow up effectiveness

  b. Pitfalls to avoid
1. *Taking things for granted* – A statement of the situation does not necessarily imply that each of the elements is necessarily true; for example, a complaint may be invalid and biased so that all that can be taken for granted is that a complaint has been registered

2. *Considering only one side of a situation* – Wherever possible, indicate several alternatives and then point out the reasons you selected the best one
3. *Failing to indicate follow up* – Whenever your answer indicates action on your part, make certain that you will take proper follow-up action to see how successful your recommendations, procedures or actions turn out to be
4. *Taking too long in answering any single question* – Remember to time your answers properly

IX. AFTER THE TEST

Scoring procedures differ in detail among civil service jurisdictions although the general principles are the same. Whether the papers are hand-scored or graded by machine we have described, they are nearly always graded by number. That is, the person who marks the paper knows only the number – never the name – of the applicant. Not until all the papers have been graded will they be matched with names. If other tests, such as training and experience or oral interview ratings have been given, scores will be combined. Different parts of the examination usually have different weights. For example, the written test might count 60 percent of the final grade, and a rating of training and experience 40 percent. In many jurisdictions, veterans will have a certain number of points added to their grades.

After the final grade has been determined, the names are placed in grade order and an eligible list is established. There are various methods for resolving ties between those who get the same final grade – probably the most common is to place first the name of the person whose application was received first. Job offers are made from the eligible list in the order the names appear on it. You will be notified of your grade and your rank as soon as all these computations have been made. This will be done as rapidly as possible.

People who are found to meet the requirements in the announcement are called "eligibles." Their names are put on a list of eligible candidates. An eligible's chances of getting a job depend on how high he stands on this list and how fast agencies are filling jobs from the list.

When a job is to be filled from a list of eligibles, the agency asks for the names of people on the list of eligibles for that job. When the civil service commission receives this request, it sends to the agency the names of the three people highest on this list. Or, if the job to be filled has specialized requirements, the office sends the agency the names of the top three persons who meet these requirements from the general list.

The appointing officer makes a choice from among the three people whose names were sent to him. If the selected person accepts the appointment, the names of the others are put back on the list to be considered for future openings.

That is the rule in hiring from all kinds of eligible lists, whether they are for typist, carpenter, chemist, or something else. For every vacancy, the appointing officer has his choice of any one of the top three eligibles on the list. This explains why the person whose name is on top of the list sometimes does not get an appointment when some of the persons lower on the list do. If the appointing officer chooses the second or third eligible, the No. 1 eligible does not get a job at once, but stays on the list until he is appointed or the list is terminated.

X. HOW TO PASS THE INTERVIEW TEST

The examination for which you applied requires an oral interview test. You have already taken the written test and you are now being called for the interview test – the final part of the formal examination.

You may think that it is not possible to prepare for an interview test and that there are no procedures to follow during an interview. Our purpose is to point out some things you can do in advance that will help you and some good rules to follow and pitfalls to avoid while you are being interviewed.

What is an interview supposed to test?

The written examination is designed to test the technical knowledge and competence of the candidate; the oral is designed to evaluate intangible qualities, not readily measured otherwise, and to establish a list showing the relative fitness of each candidate – as measured against his competitors – for the position sought. Scoring is not on the basis of "right" and "wrong," but on a sliding scale of values ranging from "not passable" to "outstanding." As a matter of fact, it is possible to achieve a relatively low score without a single "incorrect" answer because of evident weakness in the qualities being measured.

Occasionally, an examination may consist entirely of an oral test – either an individual or a group oral. In such cases, information is sought concerning the technical knowledges and abilities of the candidate, since there has been no written examination for this purpose. More commonly, however, an oral test is used to supplement a written examination.

Who conducts interviews?

The composition of oral boards varies among different jurisdictions. In nearly all, a representative of the personnel department serves as chairman. One of the members of the board may be a representative of the department in which the candidate would work. In some cases, "outside experts" are used, and, frequently, a businessman or some other representative of the general public is asked to serve. Labor and management or other special groups may be represented. The aim is to secure the services of experts in the appropriate field.

However the board is composed, it is a good idea (and not at all improper or unethical) to ascertain in advance of the interview who the members are and what groups they represent. When you are introduced to them, you will have some idea of their backgrounds and interests, and at least you will not stutter and stammer over their names.

What should be done before the interview?

While knowledge about the board members is useful and takes some of the surprise element out of the interview, there is other preparation which is more substantive. It *is* possible to prepare for an oral interview – in several ways:

1) Keep a copy of your application and review it carefully before the interview

This may be the only document before the oral board, and the starting point of the interview. Know what education and experience you have listed there, and the sequence and dates of all of it. Sometimes the board will ask you to review the highlights of your experience for them; you should not have to hem and haw doing it.

2) Study the class specification and the examination announcement

Usually, the oral board has one or both of these to guide them. The qualities, characteristics or knowledges required by the position sought are stated in these documents. They offer valuable clues as to the nature of the oral interview. For example, if the job involves supervisory responsibilities, the announcement will usually indicate that knowledge of modern supervisory methods and the qualifications of the candidate as a supervisor will be tested. If so, you can expect such questions, frequently in the form of a hypothetical situation which you are expected to solve. NEVER go into an oral without knowledge of the duties and responsibilities of the job you seek.

3) Think through each qualification required

Try to visualize the kind of questions you would ask if you were a board member. How well could you answer them? Try especially to appraise your own knowledge and background in each area, *measured against the job sought*, and identify any areas in which you are weak. Be critical and realistic – do not flatter yourself.

4) Do some general reading in areas in which you feel you may be weak

For example, if the job involves supervision and your past experience has NOT, some general reading in supervisory methods and practices, particularly in the field of human relations, might be useful. Do NOT study agency procedures or detailed manuals. The oral board will be testing your understanding and capacity, not your memory.

5) Get a good night's sleep and watch your general health and mental attitude

You will want a clear head at the interview. Take care of a cold or any other minor ailment, and of course, no hangovers.

What should be done on the day of the interview?

Now comes the day of the interview itself. Give yourself plenty of time to get there. Plan to arrive somewhat ahead of the scheduled time, particularly if your appointment is in the fore part of the day. If a previous candidate fails to appear, the board might be ready for you a bit early. By early afternoon an oral board is almost invariably behind schedule if there are many candidates, and you may have to wait. Take along a book or magazine to read, or your application to review, but leave any extraneous material in the waiting room when you go in for your interview. In any event, relax and compose yourself.

The matter of dress is important. The board is forming impressions about you – from your experience, your manners, your attitude, and your appearance. Give your personal appearance careful attention. Dress your best, but not your flashiest. Choose conservative, appropriate clothing, and be sure it is immaculate. This is a business interview, and your appearance should indicate that you regard it as such. Besides, being well groomed and properly dressed will help boost your confidence.

Sooner or later, someone will call your name and escort you into the interview room. *This is it.* From here on you are on your own. It is too late for any more preparation. But remember, you asked for this opportunity to prove your fitness, and you are here because your request was granted.

What happens when you go in?

The usual sequence of events will be as follows: The clerk (who is often the board stenographer) will introduce you to the chairman of the oral board, who will introduce you to the other members of the board. Acknowledge the introductions before you sit down. Do not be surprised if you find a microphone facing you or a stenotypist sitting by. Oral interviews are usually recorded in the event of an appeal or other review.

Usually the chairman of the board will open the interview by reviewing the highlights of your education and work experience from your application – primarily for the benefit of the other members of the board, as well as to get the material into the record. Do not interrupt or comment unless there is an error or significant misinterpretation; if that is the case, do not hesitate. But do not quibble about insignificant matters. Also, he will usually ask you some question about your education, experience or your present job – partly to get you to start talking and to establish the interviewing "rapport." He may start the actual questioning, or turn it over to one of the other members. Frequently, each member undertakes the questioning on a particular area, one in which he is perhaps most competent, so you can expect each member to participate in the examination. Because time is limited, you may also expect some rather abrupt switches in the direction the questioning takes, so do not be upset by it. Normally, a board member will not pursue a single line of questioning unless he discovers a particular strength or weakness.

After each member has participated, the chairman will usually ask whether any member has any further questions, then will ask you if you have anything you wish to add. Unless you are expecting this question, it may floor you. Worse, it may start you off on an extended, extemporaneous speech. The board is not usually seeking more information. The question is principally to offer you a last opportunity to present further qualifications or to indicate that you have nothing to add. So, if you feel that a significant qualification or characteristic has been overlooked, it is proper to point it out in a sentence or so. Do not compliment the board on the thoroughness of their examination – they have been sketchy, and you know it. If you wish, merely say, "No thank you, I have nothing further to add." This is a point where you can "talk yourself out" of a good impression or fail to present an important bit of information. Remember, *you close the interview yourself.*

The chairman will then say, "That is all, Mr. _____, thank you." Do not be startled; the interview is over, and quicker than you think. Thank him, gather your belongings and take your leave. Save your sigh of relief for the other side of the door.

How to put your best foot forward

Throughout this entire process, you may feel that the board individually and collectively is trying to pierce your defenses, seek out your hidden weaknesses and embarrass and confuse you. Actually, this is not true. They are obliged to make an appraisal of your qualifications for the job you are seeking, and they want to see you in your best light. Remember, they must interview all candidates and a non-cooperative candidate may become a failure in spite of their best efforts to bring out his qualifications. Here are 15 suggestions that will help you:

1) Be natural – Keep your attitude confident, not cocky

If you are not confident that you can do the job, do not expect the board to be. Do not apologize for your weaknesses, try to bring out your strong points. The board is interested in a positive, not negative, presentation. Cockiness will antagonize any board member and make him wonder if you are covering up a weakness by a false show of strength.

2) Get comfortable, but don't lounge or sprawl

Sit erectly but not stiffly. A careless posture may lead the board to conclude that you are careless in other things, or at least that you are not impressed by the importance of the occasion. Either conclusion is natural, even if incorrect. Do not fuss with your clothing, a pencil or an ashtray. Your hands may occasionally be useful to emphasize a point; do not let them become a point of distraction.

3) Do not wisecrack or make small talk

This is a serious situation, and your attitude should show that you consider it as such. Further, the time of the board is limited – they do not want to waste it, and neither should you.

4) Do not exaggerate your experience or abilities
In the first place, from information in the application or other interviews and sources, the board may know more about you than you think. Secondly, you probably will not get away with it. An experienced board is rather adept at spotting such a situation, so do not take the chance.

5) If you know a board member, do not make a point of it, yet do not hide it
Certainly you are not fooling him, and probably not the other members of the board. Do not try to take advantage of your acquaintanceship – it will probably do you little good.

6) Do not dominate the interview
Let the board do that. They will give you the clues – do not assume that you have to do all the talking. Realize that the board has a number of questions to ask you, and do not try to take up all the interview time by showing off your extensive knowledge of the answer to the first one.

7) Be attentive
You only have 20 minutes or so, and you should keep your attention at its sharpest throughout. When a member is addressing a problem or question to you, give him your undivided attention. Address your reply principally to him, but do not exclude the other board members.

8) Do not interrupt
A board member may be stating a problem for you to analyze. He will ask you a question when the time comes. Let him state the problem, and wait for the question.

9) Make sure you understand the question
Do not try to answer until you are sure what the question is. If it is not clear, restate it in your own words or ask the board member to clarify it for you. However, do not haggle about minor elements.

10) Reply promptly but not hastily
A common entry on oral board rating sheets is "candidate responded readily," or "candidate hesitated in replies." Respond as promptly and quickly as you can, but do not jump to a hasty, ill-considered answer.

11) Do not be peremptory in your answers
A brief answer is proper – but do not fire your answer back. That is a losing game from your point of view. The board member can probably ask questions much faster than you can answer them.

12) Do not try to create the answer you think the board member wants
He is interested in what kind of mind you have and how it works – not in playing games. Furthermore, he can usually spot this practice and will actually grade you down on it.

13) Do not switch sides in your reply merely to agree with a board member
Frequently, a member will take a contrary position merely to draw you out and to see if you are willing and able to defend your point of view. Do not start a debate, yet do not surrender a good position. If a position is worth taking, it is worth defending.

14) Do not be afraid to admit an error in judgment if you are shown to be wrong

The board knows that you are forced to reply without any opportunity for careful consideration. Your answer may be demonstrably wrong. If so, admit it and get on with the interview.

15) Do not dwell at length on your present job

The opening question may relate to your present assignment. Answer the question but do not go into an extended discussion. You are being examined for a *new* job, not your present one. As a matter of fact, try to phrase ALL your answers in terms of the job for which you are being examined.

Basis of Rating

Probably you will forget most of these "do's" and "don'ts" when you walk into the oral interview room. Even remembering them all will not ensure you a passing grade. Perhaps you did not have the qualifications in the first place. But remembering them will help you to put your best foot forward, without treading on the toes of the board members.

Rumor and popular opinion to the contrary notwithstanding, an oral board wants you to make the best appearance possible. They know you are under pressure – but they also want to see how you respond to it as a guide to what your reaction would be under the pressures of the job you seek. They will be influenced by the degree of poise you display, the personal traits you show and the manner in which you respond.

ABOUT THIS BOOK

This book contains tests divided into Examination Sections. Go through each test, answering every question in the margin. We have also attached a sample answer sheet at the back of the book that can be removed and used. At the end of each test look at the answer key and check your answers. On the ones you got wrong, look at the right answer choice and learn. Do not fill in the answers first. Do not memorize the questions and answers, but understand the answer and principles involved. On your test, the questions will likely be different from the samples. Questions are changed and new ones added. If you understand these past questions you should have success with any changes that arise. Tests may consist of several types of questions. We have additional books on each subject should more study be advisable or necessary for you. Finally, the more you study, the better prepared you will be. This book is intended to be the last thing you study before you walk into the examination room. Prior study of relevant texts is also recommended. NLC publishes some of these in our Fundamental Series. Knowledge and good sense are important factors in passing your exam. Good luck also helps. So now study this Passbook, absorb the material contained within and take that knowledge into the examination. Then do your best to pass that exam.

EXAMINATION SECTION

EXAMINATION SECTION
TEST 1

DIRECTIONS: Each question or incomplete statement is followed by several suggested answers or completions. Select the one that BEST answers the question or completes the statement. *PRINT THE LETTER OF THE CORRECT ANSWER IN THE SPACE AT THE RIGHT.*

1. A woman in her mid-30s comes up to your desk and asks you how she can apply to work at your office. You do not know the immediate answer to that question.
   Which of the following would be the BEST way to respond to her request?
   A. Tell her what sounds like the right answer
   B. Tell her to talk to your boss and show her how to do that
   C. Explain you are not allowed to give out confidential information to the public
   D. Inform her that you do not know right now, but you will find out

   1.____

2. A person approaches the customer service desk and asks you to do something that you are ultimately unable to do.
   Which of the following should you avoid doing next?
   A. Opening your policy handbook and reading from it verbatim
   B. Clarifying why you cannot do what he or she is asking of you
   C. Crafting detailed and precise statements
   D. Giving the person alternative options

   2.____

3. When talking to someone from the public, which of the following statements would be LEAST frustrating for the customer to hear?
   A. "You'll have to…"   B. "Mr. X will be back at any moment…"
   C. "Let me see what I can do…"   D. "I'll do my best…"

   3.____

4. Your office recently received a letter from an individual expressing extreme frustration and disappointment at how it was handling the customer's problems. You have written an apology letter and are reviewing it before sending it to the customer.
   You should ensure the letter is NOT
   A. sincere   B. official
   C. personal   D. sent immediately

   4.____

5. If you are unable to provide a certain service or product with dependability and accuracy, it would be defined as a lack of
   A. courtesy   B. reliability   C. assurance   D. responsiveness

   5.____

6. As most civil service employees know, customer feedback can be, and usually is, an integral part of customer service.
   Which of the following feedback scenarios would be MOST useful to your organization?
   A. When it is an ongoing feedback system
   B. When centered on internal customers
   C. When it is focused on only a few indicators
   D. When every employee can see the feedback coming in

   6.____

7. Which of the following is the LEAST important factor in making sure a customer survey is a valuable tool for your company?
   A. Taking every precaution to ensure the survey input is maintained in a confidential manner
   B. Making sure the customers believe in the confidentiality of the survey
   C. Ensuring confidentiality by having an outside company administer the survey
   D. Making sure the employees buy in and promote the survey to customers

   7.____

8. Which of the following would NOT be considered part of the resolution process when identifying and dealing with a customers' problems?
   A. Following up with the customer after resolving the issue
   B. Listening and responding to each complaint the customer registers
   C. Giving the customer what they originally requested
   D. Promising the customer whatever you need to

   8.____

9. A customer approaches you with a complaint. You want to arrive at a fair solution to the problem.
   What is the FIRST step you should take in this situation?
   A. Immediately defend your company from any customer criticisms
   B. Listen to the customer describe their problem
   C. Ask the customer questions to confirm the type of problem they are having
   D. Determine a solution to the customer's problem(s)

   9.____

10. If you are dealing with a customer in a prompt manner when addressing their complaints or issues, which of the following are you demonstrating?
    A. Assurance   B. Empathy
    C. Responsiveness   D. Reliability

    10.____

11. Steve has recently been hired to work at the postal office in town. A customer comes into the office to complain about the number of packages of his they have lost over the past year.
    When Steve attempts to help the upset customer, what should he make sure to do FIRST?
    He should
    A. check into how legitimate the customer's complaints are and see if he can do anything about the missing packages
    B. just let the customer blow off some steam and chalk it up to an emotional outburst

    11.____

C. ask for help from his boss to see how to handle the situation
D. assume the complaints are accurate and immediately attempt to correct them

12. How should a service representative react when a customer first presents them with a request?
    A. Apologize
    B. Greet them in a friendly manner
    C. Read from the employee handbook about the request
    D. Ask the customer to clarify information

13. In order to assuage a customer's frustration, which of the following should a civil service employee demonstrate?
    A. Compassion   B. Indifference   C. Surprise   D. Agreement

14. A customer comes into the office requesting that your organization do something for them that you know is not part of organization policy.
    Your FIRST responsibility would be to
    A. pass the customer on to higher management to deal with the issue
    B. persuade the customer to believe that the organization can grant their request
    C. mold expectations so they more closely resemble what the organization can do for the customer
    D. tell the customer there is no way you can comply with their request

15. Of the following potential distractors, which one MOST prevents a civil service employee from displaying good listening skills while a customer is speaking?
    A. Cell phones or checking e-mail
    B. Asking superfluous questions
    C. Background office noise
    D. Interrupting the customer to speak with colleagues

16. If you are in a situation where you have to deliver a negative response to a customer, it is often better to say _____ instead of just saying "no"?
    A. "I will try to..."   B. "You can..."
    C. "Our policy does not allow..."   D. "I do not believe..."

17. You are working one-on-one with a customer.
    Which of the following would be the MOST appropriate body language to display?
    A. Make frowning faces
    B. Stare at a spot over the customer's shoulder
    C. Lean in toward the customer
    D. Cross your arms while they speak

18. The majority of communication in face-to-face meetings with customers is shown through
    A. word choice   B. tone
    C. clothing choice   D. body language

19. A customer angrily approaches you at your service desk and starts expressing his frustration with recent actions by your department.
   Which of the following should be your FIRST responses to the customer?
   A. Listen to the person, then express understanding and apologize for how they have been negatively affected by your department's action
   B. Interrupt them while they are speaking and tell them to calm down or you will not help them
   C. Give them an explanation of why your department took the actions they did
   D. None of the above

19.____

20. Of the following services, which one is NOT customized to a specific individual's needs?
   A. Hair salon
   B. Elementary education
   C. Computer counseling
   D. Dental care

20.____

21. Which of the following civil service employees demonstrates excellent customer service?
   A. A park ranger who minimizes public interaction and contact
   B. The Postal Service employee who sees the customer as a commodity
   C. The office clerk who spends a lot of time with customers sharing personal stories and anecdotes
   D. A DMV employee with open body language and direct communication

21.____

22. It is important to have excellent knowledge of services and products, if applicable, when interacting with consumers because
   A. you can demonstrate your knowledge and impress the customer
   B. your organization can have a higher margin of profit regardless of customer benefit
   C. the customer's needs can best be matched with appropriate services/products
   D. you can look good to your superiors and keep your job

22.____

23. A park ranger has recently been coming to a kids' camp dirty and unkempt. Even though her job requires her to be outside at ties, why should she still care about her personal appearance?
   A. To speed up her service to the public
   B. So she is seen as a professional in her field
   C. It would help her organizational skills
   D. To show her level of expertise as a park ranger

23.____

24. How could guided conversation be a positive with interacting with the public?
   A. It allows you to anticipate a person's needs and expectations.
   B. Most people know what they want even before they show up to your office.
   C. It creates the impression of friendliness.
   D. It helps time move faster.

24.____

25. In the event a conflict or crisis arises, which of the following would be considered a POOR action to take when interacting with the public?   25._____
    A. Provide a constant flow of information
    B. Put the public's needs first
    C. Avoid saying "No Comment" as much as possible
    D. Assign multiple spokespeople so media calls can be dealt with efficiently

KEY (CORRECT ANSWERS)

1.	D	11.	A
2.	A	12.	D
3.	C	13.	A
4.	B	14.	C
5.	B	15.	D
6.	A	16.	B
7.	C	17.	C
8.	D	18.	D
9.	B	19.	A
10.	C	20.	B

21.	D
22.	C
23.	B
24.	A
25.	D

TEST 2

DIRECTIONS: Each question or incomplete statement is followed by several suggested answers or completions. Select the one that BEST answers the question or completes the statement. *PRINT THE LETTER OF THE CORRECT ANSWER IN THE SPACE AT THE RIGHT.*

1. John Smith answers a caller who struggles to understand a convoluted policy of your agency.
   How should he handle the customer's question?
   A. Tell the caller to go to the agency's website
   B. He should be honest and say he does not know the answer to the question
   C. John should explain the policy in general terms and refer them to a written version of the policy
   D. Tell the caller to talk to his supervisor and then give the caller the supervisor's extension

   1.____

2. While meeting with a group of young campers at the local parks and recreation office, you conduct a lecture on the importance of avoiding dangerous plants near the forest.
   What can you do to make sure your inexperienced audience remembers the main points of your presentation?
   A. Use flashy visuals that catch the eye
   B. Repeat and emphasize your points
   C. Make jokes so the presentation is livelier
   D. Allow the campers to ask questions at the end of the presentation

   2.____

3. A park ranger is about to deliver a speech at a public conservation meeting. Which of the following is the MOST important thing to keep in mind as he preps for the presentation?
   A. How large the audience is
   B. Whether or not he will be able to use visual aids
   C. If he will have time to use charts and graphs
   D. Audience interests

   3.____

4. Jerry receives a letter from a customer and is about to shred it without reading. When you stop him, he says that there is no reason to read it because you cannot learn very much from letters you receive from the public.
   Which of the following should you tell him in order to convince him that reading letters sent from the public is beneficial and necessary?
   A. These public letters can give us a feel for how we are meeting customer needs.
   B. Letters from the public tell us how well our informational efforts are working.
   C. These letters can inform us of what additional training we may need.
   D. The letters can tell us whether public information processes need to be changed or not.

   4.____

5. Ms. Johnson is a volunteer with the Parks and Recreation Department and her children also attend various summer programs through the district. She comes to you today to complain that one of her children was not allowed to join a program because they missed the sign-up by one day. She calls your staff a bunch of "morons" and complains that your department's actions are creating serious issues for her.
   How should you handle this situation?
   A. Let Ms. Johnson rant until she gets it out of her system
   B. Tell her you cannot help her and will ask her to leave if she cannot stop referring to your colleagues as "morons"
   C. Refer Ms. Johnson to your boss
   D. Try to alter the tone of the conversation to a more objective and less emotional discussion of Ms. Johnson's problems

6. A civil service employee is tasked with moderating a town hall meeting regarding child safety, but he knows that residents will be attending the meeting with different motives.
   How can the employee make sure the town hall meeting is as beneficial and informational as possible?
   A. Ask attendees to be open to changing their opinions and preferences
   B. Start out by recognizing the various motives but also stress the common objectives and interests
   C. Call out individuals who you know have specific reasons for attending and put them on the spot
   D. Cancel the meeting and avoid rescheduling it until you can be sure everyone is on the same page

7. During the question-and-answer session at the end of a presentation, a member of the public makes a suggestion that you deem not only practical but worthy of further discussion.
   How should you react to this?
   A. Tell them you will let the appropriate people know of the suggestion
   B. Tell the person you concur with them wholeheartedly
   C. Let the person know you think it is a good idea but you cannot make decisions based on suggestions during Q and A
   D. Even though the suggestion is good, tell the person that someone in your organization has probably already thought of the idea

8. When in a conversation with a group of local residents, what is the BIGGEST problem with one or two people dominating the conversation?
   A. Your interaction could take longer than it should
   B. Some people will become distracted and not focus on the meeting anymore
   C. The other member of the group may not have an opportunity to share their opinions
   D. None of the above

9. You receive a phone call at the village hall, but the information being requested would need to come from the police station.
   How should you respond to the caller?
   A. Give them the police station's website and wish them well
   B. Tell them you are not responsible for their request
   C. Refer them to the police station's number and information
   D. Provide them with the information as best as you can

9.____

10. Which of the following should almost always be avoided when interacting with a member of the community?
    A. Contentious matters
    B. Topics about financial material
    C. Rules and regulations
    D. Technical lingo or jargon

10.____

11. When people use inflammatory language laced with obscenities, a town employee should
    A. refuse to continue the dialogue if the person cannot stop using the offensive language
    B. tell the person to talk to your supervisor
    C. allow the person to finish "venting" before attempting to find a solution to the problem
    D. hang up if on the phone; if in person, leave the area and ask the individual to leave as well

11.____

12. A member of the public has sent your agency a letter.
    Which of the following will help you figure out how much explaining you need to do when writing a response?
    A. Go to the agency website and search for how much explanation is provided there
    B. Take out the original customer letter and study it
    C. Presume the person who wrote the letter already has a working knowledge of the subject and thus will not require a lot of background explanation
    D. Look at past letters sent by your agency

12.____

13. During an informational meeting with local townspeople, a man makes a suggestion for a new town measure that is based on incorrect information and is impractical.
    What is the BEST way to handle a situation such as this?
    A. Ask if anyone else in attendance would like to respond to the suggestion
    B. Tell the person it is a great idea even though you are aware of its folly
    C. Thank the man for coming and tell everyone you always welcome their suggestions
    D. Inform the person that his/her comment clearly reflects an inferior knowledge about the subject

13.____

14. A member from the public calls your office about negative comments he has heard about one of your programs. You believe the comments were made by someone who had inaccurate material, but you are not completely certain of that because you are not directly involved with the program.

14.____

What is the BEST way to handle this situation?
- A. Tell the caller you will analyze the situation in depth and then call them back
- B. Tell the caller the evidence on which they have based their judgment is not supported
- C. Explain that your office has a "No Comment" policy regarding negative comments
- D. Let the caller know you are not involved with the program directly, and tell them to call the person who is

15. Which of the following quotes reflects the BEST way to handle an angry resident that keeps interrupting during a village meeting?   15.____
    - A. "I am here as a volunteer and I do not need this."
    - B. "I understand your anger, but we have quite a bit of information to cover tonight, so in fairness to everyone else, please let me continue."
    - C. "Every crowd has one black sheep in it."
    - D. "Sir, (or Ma'am) if you cannot stop interjecting, I will have security escort you from the premises."

16. Of the following, which is an example of nonverbal communication?   16.____
    - A. Frowning
    - B. Hand signs
    - C. A "21 Gun Salute"
    - D. All of the above

17. Residents of Masterton, Georgia, were recently made aware that the main road into and out of town will be under construction for the next four years. The construction will make travel time much more difficult for the citizens and they have demanded a meeting with your department. You are tasked with creating a presentation to explain to them why the construction is necessary.   17.____
    At the start of the presentation, you should
    - A. make a joke to lighten the mood
    - B. state the purpose of your presentation
    - C. provide a detailed account of the history behind the project
    - D. make a call to action

18. When a member of the public asks questions that are confusing or you do not understand right away, what is the BEST way to handle this situation?   18.____
    - A. Answer the question as you understand it
    - B. Stick to generalizations dealing with the subject of the question
    - C. Rephrase the question and ask the person if you understood what they were asking
    - D. Ask the person to repeat the question

19. When preparing for a public interaction, which of the following situations would be MOST appropriate to include handouts?   19.____
    - A. If you want to help the attendees remember important information after the interaction is over
    - B. If you want to keep the interaction short

C. When you want to remember key points to talk about
D. When you do not want attendees to have to pay attention during the interaction

20. John is in the process of handling a phone call when a local citizen approaches his desk to ask a question. Neither the caller nor the visitor seem to be in a crisis.
    What should John do in this scenario?
    A. Keep talking with the caller until he is finished. Then tell the visitor he is sorry for making them wait.
    B. Remain on the phone with the caller but look up at the visitor every once and awhile so they know he has not forgotten about them.
    C. Tell the caller he has a visitor, so the conversation needs to end.
    D. Tell the visitor he will be with them as soon as he finishes the phone call.

20.____

21. When engaged in conversation with another person, which communication technique is MOST likely to ensure you comprehend fully what the other person to trying to communicate to you?
    A. Repeat back to the person what you think they are communicating
    B. Continual eye contact
    C. Making sure the person speaks slowly
    D. Nodding your head while they speak

21.____

22. You encounter someone who is frustrated about a situation and needs to vent by talking it out before they can move onto a productive conversation.
    When a situation is like this, it is often BEST to
    A. recommend various strategies for calming down
    B. Ask to be excused from the conversation without offering why
    C. Explain to the person that it is unproductive to behave the way they are currently behaving
    D. Acknowledge that venting is a crucial step to moving past the emotions and allow the person to express his or her feelings

23.____

23. Which of the following is NOT an example of active listening?
    A. Taking notes
    B. Referring the customer to the manager after they are done speaking
    C. Using phrases like "I see" or "Go on"
    D. Repeating back to the customer what you've heard

23.____

24. Which of the following questions would be classified as a clarification question?
    A. "How long have you sold spoiled meat?"
    B. "Do you like our brand?"
    C. "You mentioned you liked this merchandise. How would you feel about this?"
    D. None of the above

24.____

25. When interacting with a member of the public, which of the following words should you avoid using as it is not positive as perceived by most people? 25.____
    A. "Absolutely"
    B. "You are welcome"
    C. "Here's what I can do"
    D. "I'll do my best"

KEY (CORRECT ANSWERS)

1.	C		11.	A
2.	B		12.	B
3.	D		13.	C
4.	A		14.	A
5.	D		15.	B
6.	B		16.	D
7.	A		17.	B
8.	C		18.	C
9.	C		19.	A
10.	D		20.	D

21. A
22. D
23. B
24. C
25. D

EXAMINATION SECTION
TEST 1

DIRECTIONS: Each question or incomplete statement is followed by several suggested answers or completions. Select the one that BEST answers the question or completes the statement. *PRINT THE LETTER OF THE CORRECT ANSWER IN THE SPACE AT THE RIGHT.*

1. Companies with successful customer service organizations usually experience each of the following EXCEPT
    A. fewer customer complaints
    B. greater response to advertising
    C. lower marketing costs
    D. more repeat business

2. To be most useful to an organization, feedback received from customers should be each of the following EXCEPT
    A. centered on internal customers
    B. orgoing
    C. focused on a limited number of indicators
    D. available to every employee in the organization

3. Instead of directly saying *no* to a customer, service representatives will usually get BEST results with a reply that begins with the words:
    A. I'll try
    B. I don't believe
    C. You can
    D. It's not our policy

4. Once a customer problem is identified, each of the following should become a part of the service recovery process EXCEPT
    A. following up on the problem resolution
    B. making whatever promises are necessary
    C. providing the customer with what was originally requested
    D. listening and responding to every complaint given by the customer

5. The percentage of an organization's annual business that involves repeat customers is CLOSEST to
    A. 25%   B. 45%   C. 65%   D. 85%

6. Of the following, the _____ is NOT generally considered to be a major source of *service promise*.
    A. customer service representative
    B. organization
    C. particular department that delivers product to the customer
    D. customer

7. A customer appears to be mildly irritated when lodging a complaint. The MOST appropriate action for a service representative to take while attempting resolution is to
   A. allow venting of frustrations
   B. enlist the customer in generating solutions
   C. show emotional neutrality
   D. create calm

8. If an organization loses one customer who normally spends $50 per week, the projected result of reduction in sales for the following year will be APPROXIMATELY
   A. $2,600   B. $12,400   C. $124,000   D. $950,000

9. The majority of *service promises* originate from
   A. organizational management
   B. customer service professionals
   C. the customers' expectations
   D. organizational marketing

10. To arrive at a *fair fix* to a service problem, one should FIRSTS
    A. offer an apology for the problem
    B. ask probing questions to understand and confirm the nature of the problem
    C. listen to the customer's description of the problem
    D. determine and implement a solution to the problem

11. Which of the following is NOT generally considered to be a function of *open questioning* when dealing with a customer?
    A. Defining problems
    B. Confirming an order
    C. Getting more information
    D. Establishing customer needs

12. When dealing with a customer, service representatives should generally use the pronoun
    A. *they*, meaning the company as a whole
    B. *they*, meaning the department to whom the complaint will be referred
    C. *I*, meaning themselves, as representatives of the organization
    D. *we*, meaning themselves and the customer

13. A customer service representative demonstrates product and service knowledge by
    A. anticipating the changing needs of customers
    B. soliciting feedback from customers about customer service
    C. studying the capabilities of the office computer system
    D. knowing what questions are asked most by customers about a product or service

14. When listening to a customer during a face-to-face meeting, the MOST appropriate non-verbal gesture is
    A. clenched fists
    B. leaning slightly toward a customer
    C. hands casually in pockets
    D. standing with crossed arms

15. Before breaking or bending an existing service rule in order to better serve a customer, a representative should be aware of each of the following EXCEPT the
    A. reason for the rule
    B. location of a written copy of the rule and policy
    C. consequences of not following the rule
    D. situations in which the rule is applicable

    15.____

16. The LEAST likely reason for a dissatisfied customer's failure to complain about a product or service is that the customer
    A. does not think the complaint will produce the desired results
    B. is unaware of the proper channels through which to voice his/her complaint
    C. does not believe he/she has the time to spend on the complaint
    D. does not believe anyone in the organization really cares about the complaint

    16.____

17. Most research shows that _____% of what is communicated between people during face-to-face meetings is conveyed through entirely nonverbal cues.
    A. 10   B. 30   C. 50   D. 80

    17.____

18. When a customer submits a written complaint, the representative should write a response that avoids
    A. addressing every single component of the customer's complaint
    B. a personal tone
    C. the use of a pre-formulated response structure
    D. mentioning future business transactions

    18.____

19. A customer service representative spends several hours practicing with the various forms and paperwork required by the company for handling customer service situations.
    Which of the following basic areas of learning is the representative trying to improve upon?
    A. Interpersonal skills   B. Product and service knowledge
    C. Customer knowledge   D. Technical skills

    19.____

20. If a customer service representative must deal with other members of a service team in order to resolve a problem, the representative should avoid
    A. developing personal relationships
    B. giving others credit for ideas that clearly were not theirs
    C. circumventing uncooperative team members by quietly contacting a superior
    D. involving customers in the resolution of a complaint

    20.____

21. A customer service representative is willing to help customers promptly.
    Which of the following service factors is the representative able to demonstrate?
    A. Assurance   B. Responsiveness
    C. Empathy   D. Reliability

    21.____

22. A service representative begins work in a specialized order entry job and son learns that many customers call in with orders at the last minute, causing her routine to be thrown out of balance and creating stress.
After studying the ordering patterns of all clients, the MOST effective resolution to the problem would be to
    A. mail reminder notices to habitually late customers in advance of typical ordering dates to establish lead time
    B. telephone habitually late customers a few days before their typical ordering dates to establish lead time
    C. place the orders of habitually late customers in advance, changing them later if necessary
    D. establish and enforce a rigid lead-time deadline to create more manageable client behavior

22.____

23. For BEST results, customer service representatives will improve service by considering themselves to be representative of
    A. the entire organization
    B. the department receiving the complaint
    C. the customer
    D. an adversary of the organization, who will fight along with the customer

23.____

24. Of all the customers who stop doing business with organizations, _____% do so because of product dissatisfaction.
    A. 15   B. 40   C. 65   D. 80

24.____

25. When using the *problem-solving* approach to solve the problem of a dissatisfied customer, the LAST step should be to
    A. double check for customer satisfaction
    B. identify the customer's expectations
    C. outline a solution or alternatives
    D. take action on the problem

25.____

KEY (CORRECT ANSWERS)

1.	B	11.	B
2.	A	12.	C
3.	C	13.	D
4.	B	14.	B
5.	C	15.	B
6.	C	16.	C
7.	B	17.	C
8.	A	18.	C
9.	B	19.	D
10.	C	20.	C

21. B
22. B
23. A
24. A
25. A

TEST 2

DIRECTIONS: Each question or incomplete statement is followed by several suggested answers or completions. Select the one that BEST answers the question or completes the statement. *PRINT THE LETTER OF THE CORRECT ANSWER IN THE SPACE AT THE RIGHT.*

1. Of the following, the LEAST likely reason for a customer to telephone an organization or department is to
    A. voice an objection
    B. make a statement
    C. offer praise
    D. ask a question

    1.____

2. Customer service usually requires each of the following EXCEPT
    A. product knowledge
    B. friendliness and approachability
    C. problem-solving skills
    D. company/organization knowledge

    2.____

3. According to research, a typical dissatisfied customer will tell about _____ people how dissatisfied he/she is with an organization's product or service.
    A. 3   B. 5   C. 10   D. 20

    3.____

4. When a service target is provided by manager, it is MOST important for a service representative to know the
    A. nature of the customer database associated with the target
    B. formula for achieving the target
    C. methods used by other service personnel for achieving the target
    D. purpose behind the target

    4.____

5. Typically, customers cause about _____ of the service and product problems they complain about.
    A. 1/5   B. 1/3   C. 1/2   D. 2/3

    5.____

6. When a dissatisfied customer complains to a service representative, making a sale is NOT considered to be good service when the
    A. customer appreciates being changed to a different service or product
    B. the original product or service is in need of additional parts or components to be complete
    C. the customer remains angry about the original complaint
    D. the original product or service is in need of repair

    6.____

7. As service representatives, personnel would be LEAST likely to be responsible for
    A. service
    B. marketing
    C. problem-solving
    D. sales

    7.____

8. When writing a memorandum on a customer complaint, _____ can be considered optional by a service representative.
    A. the date the complaint was filed and/or the problem occurred
    B. a summary of the customer's comments
    C. the address of the customer
    D. a suggestion for correcting the situation

    8.____

9. In most successful organizations, customer service is considered PRIMARILY to be the domain of the
    A. entire organization
    B. sales department
    C. complaint department
    D. service department

10. According to MOST research, the cost of attracting a new customer, in relation to the cost of retaining a current customer, is about
    A. half as much
    B. about the same
    C. twice as much
    D. five times as much

11. If a customer service representative is unable to do what a customer asks, the representative should avoid
    A. quoting organizational policy regarding the customer's request
    B. explaining why it cannot be done
    C. making specific statements
    D. offering alternatives

12. When a customer presents a service representative with a request, the representative's FIRST reaction should usually be a(n)
    A. apology
    B. friendly greeting
    C. statement of organizational policy regarding the request
    D. request for clarifying information

13. It is NOT a primary reason for written communication with customers to
    A. create documentation
    B. solidify relationships
    C. confirm understanding
    D. solicit business contact

14. Of the following, which would be LEAST frustrating for a customer to hear from a service representative?
    A. You will have to
    B. I will do my best
    C. Let me see what I can do
    D. He/she should be back any minute

15. A customer appears to be mildly irritated when lodging a complaint. It is MOST appropriate for a service representative to demonstrate _____ in reaction to the complaint.
    A. urgency   B. empathy   C. nonchalance   D. surprise

16. The _____ would be indirectly served by an individual who takes customer orders at an organization's telephone center.
    A. customer
    B. management personnel
    C. billing agents
    D. warehouse staff

17. Based on the actions of a customer service representative, customers will be MOST likely to make judgments concerning each of the following EXCEPT the
    A. kind of people employed by the organization
    B. company's value system
    C. organization's commitment to advertised promises
    D. value of the organization's product

18. When dealing with customers, a service representative's apologies, if necessary, should NOT be
    A. immediate   B. official   C. sincere   D. personal

19. Of all the customers who stop doing business with organizations, approximately _____ do so because of indifferent treatment by employees.
    A. 20%   B. 45%   C. 70%   D. 95%

20. If a customer service representative is aware that the organization is not capable of meeting a customer's expectations, the representative's FIRST responsibility would be to
    A. tell the customer of the organization's inability to comply
    B. shape the customer's expectations to match what the organization can do as he/she asks
    C. encourage the customer to believe that the organization can do as he/she asks
    D. make the sale on the organization's product

21. The following is an example of a *bonus benefit* associated with a product or service:
    A customer
    A. buys a sporty sedan and finds that its tight turning ratio makes it easy to park
    B. buys bread specifically because he wants to receive a coupon for his next purchase
    C. purchases a car and discovers a strange smell in the upholstery
    D. buys a music audiotape and discovers that there are advertisements at the beginning and end of the tape

22. Approximately _____ of customers who voice complaints with an organization will continue to do business with the organization if the complaint is resolved promptly.
    A. 25   B. 40   C. 75   D. 95

23. Though necessary, a positive, proactive customer satisfaction policy will USUALLY be restricted by costs and
    A. volume of service problems
    B. limitations of management personnel authority
    C. unreasonable customer demands
    D. limitations of service policy

24. According to MOST customers, _____ prevents good listening on the part of a service representative when a customer is speaking.
    A. technological apparatus (e.g., voicemail)
    B. frequent interruptions by other staff or customers
    C. asking unnecessary questions
    D. background noise

25. The ability to provide the promised service or product dependably and accurately maybe defined as
    A. assurance
    B. responsiveness
    C. courtesy
    D. reliability

25.____

KEY (CORRECT ANSWERS)

1. C
2. B
3. C
4. D
5. B

6. C
7. B
8. C
9. A
10. D

11. A
12. D
13. D
14. C
15. A

16. B
17. D
18. B
19. C
20. B

21. A
22. D
23. D
24. B
25. D

EXAMINATION SECTION
TEST 1

DIRECTIONS: Each question or incomplete statement is followed by several suggested answers or completions. Select the one that BEST answers the question or completes the statement. *PRINT THE LETTER OF THE CORRECT ANSWER IN THE SPACE AT THE RIGHT.*

1. Public organizations usually share each of the following customer-service problems with private organizations EXCEPT
    A. aversion to risk
    B. staff-heaviness
    C. provision of reverse incentives
    D. control-apportionment functions

2. A service representative demonstrates interpersonal skills by
    A. identifying a customer's expectations
    B. learning how to use a new office telephone system
    C. studying a competitor's approach to service
    D. anticipating how a customer will react to certain situations

3. Of the following, _____ is NOT generally considered to be a common reason for flaws in an organization's customer focus.
    A. commissioned employee compensation
    B. full problem-solving authority for front-line personnel
    C. inadequate hiring practices
    D. specific, case-oriented policy and procedural statements

4. According to MOST research, approximately _____ of dissatisfied customers will actually complain or make their dissatisfaction with a product known to the organization.
    A. 5%   B. 25%   C. 50%   D. 75%

5. Which of the following is an example of an expected benefit associated with a product or service?
    A. Before buying a car, a customer believes she will not have to take the car in for repairs every few months.
    B. A customer in a sporting goods store tells a salesperson exactly what kind of trolling motor will meet the requirements of the lakes the customer wanted to fish.
    C. A supermarket shopper buys a loaf of bread, believing that the bread will remain fresh for a few days.
    D. An airline passenger discover that the meals served on board are good.

6. During a meeting with a service representative, a customer makes an apparently reasonable request. However, the representative knows that satisfying the customer's request will violate a rule that is part of the organization's policy. Although the representative feels that an exception to the rule should be made in this case, she is not sure whether an exception can or should be made.

The BEST course of action for the representative would be to
A. deny the request and apologize, explaining the company policy
B. rely on good judgment and allow the request
C. try to steer the customer toward a similar but clearly permissible request
D. contact a manager or more experienced peer to handle the request

7. While organizing an effective customer service department, it would be LEAST effective to
   A. create procedures for relaying reasons for complaints to other departments
   B. set up a clear chain-of-command for handling specific customer complaints
   C. continually monitor performance of front-line personnel
   D. give front-line people full authority to resolve all customer dissatisfaction

8. Of the following, _____ is an example of *tangible* service.
   A. an interior decorator telling his/her ideas to a potential client
   B. a salesclerk giving a written cost estimate to a potential buyer
   C. an automobile salesman telling a showroom customer about a car's performance
   D. a stockbroker offering investment advice over the telephone

9. As a rule, a customer service representative who handles telephones should always answer a call within no more than _____ ring(s).
   A. 1   B. 3   C. 5   D. 8

10. In order to be as useful as possible to an organization, feedback received from customers should NOT be
    A. portrayed on a line graph or similar device
    B. used to provide a general overview
    C. focused on end-use customers
    D. available upon demand

11. Of all the customers who switch to competing organizations approximately _____ percent do so because of poor service.
    A. 25   B. 40   C. 75   D. 95

12. When customers offer information that is incorrect in their complaints, a service representative should do each of the following EXCEPT
    A. assume that the customer is making an innocent mistake
    B. look for opportunities to educate the customer
    C. calmly state a reasonable argument that will correct the customer's mistake
    D. believe the customer until he/she is able to find proof of his/her error

13. In order to insure that a customer feels comfortable in a face-to-face meeting, a service representative should
    A. avoid discussing controversial issues
    B. use personal terms such as *dear* or *friend*
    C. address the customer by his/her first name
    D. tell a few jokes

14. Customer satisfaction is MOST effectively measured in terms of
    A. cost   B. benefit   C. convenience   D. value

15. Making a sale is NOT considered good service when
    A. there are no alternatives to the subject of the customer's complaint
    B. when the original product or service is outdated
    C. an add-in feature will forestall other problems
    D. the product or service the customer has been using is the wrong product

16. When dealing with an indecisive customer, the service representative should
    A. expand available possibilities
    B. offer a way out of unsatisfying decisions
    C. ask probing questions for understanding
    D. steer the customer toward one particular decision

17. Of the following, _____ would NOT be a source of direct organizational service promises.
    A. advertising materials
    B. published organizational policies
    C. contracts
    D. the customer's past experience with the organization

18. Generally, the only kind of organization that can validly circumvent the requirements of customer service is one that
    A. cannot afford to staff an entire service department
    B. relies solely on the sale of ten or fewer items per year
    C. has little or no competition
    D. serves clients that are separated from consumers

19. When using the problem-solving approach to solve the problem of an upset customer, the service representative should FIRST
    A. express respect for the customer
    B. identify the customer's expectations
    C. outline a solution or alternatives
    D. listen to understand the problem

20. During face-to-face meetings with strangers such as service personnel, most North Americans consider a comfortable proximity to be
    A. 6 inches - 1 foot   B. 8 inches - 1½ feet
    C. 1½ - 2 feet   D. 2-4 feet

21. When answering phone calls, a service representative should ALWAYS do each of the following EXCEPT
    A. state his/her name
    B. give the name of the organization or department
    C. ask probing questions
    D. offer assistance

22. If a customer appears to be emotionally neutral when lodging a complaint, it would be MOST appropriate for a service representative to demonstrate ____ in reaction to the complaint.
    A. urgency   B. empathy   C. nonchalance   D. surprise

23. When soliciting customer feedback, standard practice is to limit the number of questions asked to APPROXIMATELY
    A. 3-5   B. 5-10   C. 10-20   D. 15-40

24. A customer has purchased an item from a company and has been told that the item will be delivered in two weeks. However, a customer service representative later discovers that deliveries are running about three days behind schedule.
    The MOST appropriate course of action for the representative would be to
    A. call the customer immediately, apologize for the delay, and await the customer's response
    B. call the customer a few days before delivery is due and explain that the delay is the fault of the delivery company
    C. immediately sent out a *loaner* of the ordered item to the customer
    D. wait for the customer to note the delay and contact the organization

25. Most research show that ____% of what is communicated between people during face-to-face meetings is conveyed through words alone.
    A. 10   B. 30   C. 50   D. 80

KEY (CORRECT ANSWERS)

1.	D	11.	B
2.	D	12.	C
3.	B	13.	A
4.	A	14.	D
5.	B	15.	A
6.	D	16.	B
7.	B	17.	D
8.	B	18.	C
9.	B	19.	A
10.	B	20.	C

21. C
22. D
23. B
24. A
25. A

TEST 2

DIRECTIONS: Each question or incomplete statement is followed by several suggested answers or completions. Select the one that BEST answers the question or completes the statement. *PRINT THE LETTER OF THE CORRECT ANSWER IN THE SPACE AT THE RIGHT.*

1. When working cooperatively to identify specific internal service targets, personnel typically encounter each of the following obstacles EXCEPT
    A. rapidly-changing work environment
    B. philosophical differences about the nature of service
    C. specialized knowledge of certain personnel exceeds that of others
    D. a chain-of-command that isolates the end user

    1._____

2. Which of the following is an example of an external customer relationship?
    A. Baggage clerks to travelers
    B. Catering staff to flight attendants
    C. Managers to ticketing agents
    D. Maintenance workers to ground crew

    2._____

3. When a service representative puts a customer's complaint in writing, results will be produced more quickly than if the representative had merely told someone.
   Which of the following is NOT generally considered to be a reason for this?
    A. The complaint can be more easily routed to parties capable of solving the problem.
    B. Management will understand the problem more clearly.
    C. The representative can more clearly see the main aspects of the complaint.
    D. The complaint and response will become a part of a public record.

    3._____

4. A customer service representative creates a client file, which contains notes about what particular clients want, need, and expect.
   Which of the following basic areas of learning is the representative exercising?
    A. Interpersonal skills   B. Product and service knowledge
    C. Customer knowledge   D. Technical skills

    4._____

5. A customer complains that a desired product, which is currently on sale, is needed in at least two weeks, but the company is out of stock and the product will not be available for another four weeks.
   Of the following, the BEST example of a service *recovery* on the part of a representative would be to
    A. apologize for the company's inability to serve the customer while expressing a wish to deal with the customer in the future
    B. attempt to steer the customer's interest toward an unrelated product
    C. offer a comparable model at the same sale price

    5._____

6. Of the following, _____ is NOT generally considered to be a function of closed questioning when dealing with a customer.
    A. understanding requests
    B. getting the customer to agree
    C. clarifying what has been said
    D. summarizing a conversation

7. When dealing with a customer who speaks with a heavy foreign accent, a service representative should NOT
    A. speak loudly
    B. speak slowly
    C. avoid humor or witticism
    D. repeat what has been said

8. If a customer service representative is aware that time will be a factor in the delivery of service to a customer, the representative should FIRST
    A. warn the customer that the organization is under time constraints
    B. suggest that the customer return another time
    C. ask the customer to suggest a service deadline
    D. tell the customer when service can reasonably be expected

9. In relation to a customer service representative's view of an organization, the customer's view of the company tends to be
    A. more negative
    B. more objective
    C. broader in scope
    D. less forgiving

10. When asked to define the factors that determine whether they will do business with an organization, most customers maintain that _____ is the MOST important.
    A. friendly employees
    B. having their needs met
    C. convenience
    D. product pricing

11. While a customer is stating her service requirements, a service representative should do each of the following EXCEPT
    A. ask questions about complex or unclear information
    B. formulate a response to the customer's remarks
    C. repeat critical information
    D. attempt to roughly outline the customer's main points

12. If a customer service representative must deal with other member of a service team in order to resolve a problem, the representative should avoid
    A. conveying every single detail of a problem to others
    B. suggesting deadlines for problem resolution
    C. offering opinions about the source of the problem
    D. explaining the specifics concerning the need for resolution

13. Of the following, the LAST step in the resolution of a service problem should be
    A. the offer of an apology for the problem
    B. asking probing questions to understand and conform the nature of the problem
    C. listening to the customer's description of the problem
    D. determining and implementing a solution to the problem

14. _____ is a poor scheduling strategy for a customer service representative.
    A. Performing the easiest tasks first
    B. Varying work routines
    C. Setting deadlines that will allow some restful work periods
    D. Doing similar jobs at the same time

15. The MOST defensible reason for the avoidance of customer satisfaction guarantees is
    A. buyer remorse
    B. repeated customer contact
    C. high costs
    D. ability of buyers to take advantage of guarantees

16. A customer service representative demonstrates knowledge and courtesy to customers and is able to convey trust, competence, and confidence.
    Of the following service factors, the representative is demonstrating
    A. assurance   B. responsiveness
    C. empathy   D. reliability

17. If a service representative is involved in sales, _____ is NOT one of the primary pieces of information he/she will need to supply the customer.
    A. cost of product or service   B. how the product works
    C. how to repair the product   D. available payment plans

18. A customer appears to be experiencing extreme feelings of anger and frustration when loading a complaint.
    The MOST appropriate reaction for a service representative to demonstrate is
    A. urgency   B. empathy   C. nonchalance   D. surprise

19. Of the following obstacles to customer service, _____ is NOT generally considered to be unique to public organizations.
    A. ambivalence toward clients   B. limited competition
    C. a rule-based mission   D. clients who are not really customers

20. Most customers report that the MOST frustrating aspect of waiting in line for service is
    A. not knowing how long they will have to wait for service
    B. rudeness on the part of the service representatives
    C. being expected to wait for service at all
    D. unfair prioritizing on the part of service representatives

21. Which of the following is an example of an *assumed benefit* associated with a product or service?
    A customer
    A buys a sporty sedan and finds that its tight turning ratio makes it easy to park
    B. visits a fast-food restaurant because she is in a hurry to get dinner over with

4 (#2)

    C. buys a videotape and believes it will not cause damage to her VCR
    D. tells a salesman that he wants to purchase a high-status automobile

22. On an average, for every complaint received by an organization, there are actually about _____ customers who have legitimate problems.   22._____
    A. 3   B. 5   C. 15   D. 25

23. Once a customer problem is identified, each of the following should become a part of the service recovery process EXCEPT   23._____
    A. apologizing
    B. an offer of compensation
    C. empathetic listening
    D. sympathy

24. As a rule, customers who telephone organizations should not be put on hold for any longer than   24._____
    A. 10 seconds
    B. 60 seconds
    C. 5 minutes
    D. 10 minutes

25. The LEAST effective way to make customers feel as if they are a part of a service team would be to ask them for   25._____
    A. information about similar products/services they have used
    B. opinions about how to solve problems
    C. personally contact the department that can best help them
    D. opinions about particular products and services

KEY (CORRECT ANSWERS)

1.	B		11.	B
2.	A		12.	C
3.	D		13.	A
4.	C		14.	A
5.	D		15.	B
6.	A		16.	A
7.	A		17.	C
8.	C		18.	B
9.	C		19.	B
10.	B		20.	A

21. C
22. D
23. D
24. B
25. C

EXAMINATION SECTION

TEST 1

DIRECTIONS: Each question or incomplete statement is followed by several suggested answers or completions. Select the one that BEST answers the question or completes the statement. *PRINT THE LETTER OF THE CORRECT ANSWER IN THE SPACE AT THE RIGHT.*

1. A multi-line telephone with buttons for eight separate lines, plus a *hold* button, is often used when an office requires more than one outside line.
   If you are talking on one line of this type of office phone when another call comes in, what is the procedure to follow if you want to answer the second call but keep the first call on the line?
   Push the
   A. *hold* button at the same time as you push the *pickup* button of the ringing line
   B. *hold* button and then push the *pickup* button of the ringing line
   C. *pickup* button of the ringing line and then push the *hold* button
   D. *pickup* button of the ringing line and push the *hold* button when you return to the original line

   1._____

2. Suppose that you are asked to prepare a petty cash statement for March. The original and one copy are to go to the personnel office. One copy is to go to the fiscal office, and another copy is to go to your supervisor. The last copy is for your files.
   In preparing the statement and the copies, how many sheets of copy paper should you use?
   A. 3　　　　B. 4　　　　C. 5　　　　D. 8

   2._____

3. Which one of the following is the LEAST important advantage of putting the subject of a letter in the heading to the right of the address? It
   A. makes filing of the copy easier
   B. makes more space available in the body of the letter
   C. simplifies distribution of letters
   D. simplifies determination of the subject of the letter

   3._____

4. Of the following, the MOST efficient way to put 100 copies of a one-page letter into 9½" x 4⅛" envelopes for mailing is to fold _____ into an envelope.
   A. each letter and insert it immediately after folding
   B. each letter separately until all 100 are folded; then insert each one
   C. the 100 letters two at a time, then separate them and insert each one
   D. two letters together, slip them apart, and insert each one

   4._____

5. When preparing papers for filing, it is NOT desirable to
   A. smooth papers that are wrinkled
   B. use paper clips to keep related papers together in the files
   C. arrange the papers in the order in which they will be filed
   D. mend torn papers with cellophane tape

6. Of the following, the BEST reason for a clerical unit to have its own duplicating machine is that the unit
   A. uses many forms which it must reproduce internally
   B. must make two copies of each piece of incoming mail for a special file
   C. must make seven copies of each piece of outgoing mail
   D. must type 200 envelopes each month for distribution to the same offices

7. Several offices use the same photocopying machine.
   If each office must pay its share of the cost of running this machine, the BEST way of determining how much of this cost should be charged to each of these offices is to
   A. determine the monthly number of photocopies made by each office
   B. determine the monthly number of originals submitted for photocopying by each office
   C. determine the number of times per day each office uses the photocopying machine
   D. divide the total cost of running the photocopy machine by the total number of offices using the machine

8. Which one of the following would it be BEST to use to indicate that a file folder has been removed from the files for temporary use in another office?
   A(n)
   A. cross-reference card   B. tickler file marker
   C. aperture card   D. out guide

9. Which one of the following is the MOST important objective of filing?
   A. Giving a secretary something to do in her spare time
   B. Making it possible to locate information quickly
   C. Providing a place to store unneeded documents
   D. Keeping extra papers from accumulating on workers' desks

10. If a check has been made out for an incorrect amount, the BEST action for the writer of the check to take is to
    A. erase the original amount and enter the correct amount
    B. cross out the original amount with a single line and enter the correct amount above it
    C. black out the original amount so that it cannot be read and enter the correct amount above it
    D. write a new check

11. Which one of the following BEST describes the usual arrangement of a tickler file? 11.____
    A. Alphabetical   B. Chronological
    C. Numerical   D. Geographical

12. Which one of the following is the LEAST desirable filing practice? 12.____
    A. Using staples to keep papers together
    B. Filing all material without regard to date
    C. Keeping a record of all materials removed from the files
    D. Writing filing instructions on each paper prior to filing

13. Assume that one of your duties is to keep records of the office supplies used by your unit for the purpose of ordering new supplies when the old supplies run out. 13.____
    The information that will be of MOST help in letting you know when to reorder supplies is the
    A. quantity issued   B. quantity received
    C. quantity on hand   D. stock number

Questions 14-19.

DIRECTIONS: Questions 14 through 19 consist of sets of names and addresses. In each question, the name and address in Column II should be an exact copy of the name and address in Column I. If there is
a mistake *only* in the name, mark your answer A;
a mistake *only* in the address, mark your answer B;
a mistake in *both* name and address, mark your answer C;
no mistake in either name or address, mark your answer D.

SAMPLE QUESTION

Column I
Michael Filbert
456 Reade Street
New York, N.Y. 10013

Column II
Michael Filbert
645 Reade Street
New York, N.Y. 10013

Since there is a mistake only in the address (the street number should be 456 instead of 645), the answer to the sample question is B.

COLUMN I   COLUMN II

14. Esta Wong   Esta Wang   14.____
    141 West 68 St.   141 West 68 St.
    New York, N.Y. 10023   New York,, N.Y. 10023

15. Dr. Alberto Grosso   Dr. Alberto Grosso   15.____
    3475 12th Avenue   3475 12th Avenue
    Brooklyn, N.Y. 11218   Brooklyn, N.Y. 11218

	Column I	Column II	

16. Mrs. Ruth Bortlas
    482 Theresa Ct.
    Far Rockaway, N.Y. 11691

    Ms. Ruth Bortlas
    482 Theresa Ct.
    Far Rockaway, N.Y. 11169   16.____

17. Mr. and Mrs. Howard Fox
    2301 Sedgwick Avenue
    Bronx, N.Y. 10468

    Mr. and Mrs. Howard Fox
    231 Sedgwick Ave.
    Bronx, N.Y. 10458   17.____

18. Miss Marjorie Black
    223 East 23 Street
    New York, N.Y. 10010

    Miss Margorie Black
    223 East 23 Street
    New York, N.Y. 10010   18.____

19. Michelle Herman
    806 Valley Rd.
    Old Tappan, N.J. 07675

    Michelle Hermann
    806 Valley Dr.
    Old Tappan, N.J. 07675   19.____

Questions 20-25.

DIRECTIONS: Questions 20 through 25 are to be answered SOLELY on the basis of the information in the following passage.

Basic to every office is the need for proper lighting. Inadequate lighting is a familiar cause of fatigue and serves to create a somewhat dismal atmosphere in the office. One requirement of proper lighting is that it be of an appropriate intensity. Intensity is measured in foot-candles. According to the Illuminating Engineering Society of New York, for casual seeing tasks such as in reception rooms, inactive file rooms, and other service areas, it is recommended that the amount of light be 30 foot-candles. For ordinary seeing tasks such as reading and work in active file rooms and in mail rooms, the recommended lighting is 100 foot-candles. For very difficult seeing tasks such as accounting, transcribing, and business machine use, the recommended lighting is 150 foot-candles.

Lighting intensity is only one requirement. Shadows and glare are to be avoided. For example, the larger the proportion of a ceiling filled with lighting units, the more glare-free and comfortable the lighting will be. Natural lighting from windows is not too dependable because on dark wintry days, windows yield little usable light, and on sunny afternoons, the glare from windows may be very distracting. Desks should not face the windows. Finally, the main lighting source ought to be overhead and to the left of the user.

20. According to the above passage, insufficient light in the office may cause   20.____
    A. glare   B. shadows   C. tiredness   D. distraction

21. Based on the above passage, which of the following must be considered when planning lighting arrangements?   21.____
    The
    A. amount of natural light present
    B. amount of work to be done
    C. level of difficulty of work to be done
    D. type of activity to be carried out

22. It can be inferred from the above passage that a well-coordinated lighting scheme is LIKELY to result in
    A. greater employee productivity
    B. elimination of light reflection
    C. lower lighting cost
    D. more use of natural light

23. Of the following, the BEST title for the above passage is
    A. Characteristics of Light
    B. Light Measurement Devices
    C. Factors to Consider When Planning Lighting Systems
    D. Comfort vs. Cost When Devising Lighting Arrangements

24. According to the above passage, a foot-candle is a measurement of the
    A. number of bulbs used
    B. strength of the light
    C. contrast between glare and shadow
    D. proportion of the ceiling filled with lighting units

25. According to the above passage, the number of foot-candles of light that would be needed to copy figures onto a payroll is _____ foot-candles.
    A. less than 30   B. 30   C. 100   D. 150

KEY (CORRECT ANSWERS)

1. B
2. B
3. B
4. A
5. B

6. A
7. A
8. D
9. B
10. D

11. B
12. B
13. C
14. A
15. D

16. C
17. B
18. A
19. C
20. C

21. D
22. A
23. C
24. B
25. D

TEST 2

DIRECTIONS: Each question or incomplete statement is followed by several suggested answers or completions. Select the one that BEST answers the question or completes the statement. *PRINT THE LETTER OF THE CORRECT ANSWER IN THE SPACE AT THE RIGHT.*

1. Assume that a supervisor has three subordinates who perform clerical tasks. One of the employees retires and is replaced by someone who is transferred from another unit in the agency. The transferred employee tells the supervisor that she has worked as a clerical employee for two years and understands clerical operations quite well. The supervisor then assigns the transferred employee to a desk, tells the employee to begin working, and returns to his own desk.
The supervisor's action in this situation is
   A. *proper*; experienced clerical employees do not require training when they are transferred to new assignments
   B. *improper*; before the supervisor returns to his desk, he should tell the other two subordinates to watch the transferred employee perform the work
   C. *proper*; if the transferred employee makes any mistakes, she will bring them to the supervisor's attention
   D. *improper*; the supervisor should find out what clerical tasks the transferred employee has performed and give her instruction in those which are new or different

1.____

2. Assume that you are falling behind in completing your work assignments and you believe that your workload is too heavy.
Of the following, the BEST course of action for you to take FIRST is to
   A. discuss the problem with your supervisor
   B. decide which of your assignments can be postponed
   C. try to get some of your co-workers to help you out
   D. plan to take some of the work home with you in order to catch up

2.____

3. Suppose that one of the clerks under your supervision is filling in monthly personnel forms. She asks you to explain a particular personnel regulation which is related to various items on the forms. You are not thoroughly familiar with the regulation.
Of the following responses you may make, the one which will gain the MOST respect from the clerk and which is generally the MOST advisable is to
   A. tell the clerk to do the best she can and that you will check her work later
   B. inform the clerk that you are not sure of a correct explanation but suggest a procedure for her to follow
   C. give the clerk a suitable interpretation so that she will think you are familiar with all regulations
   D. tell the clerk that you will have to read the regulation more thoroughly before you can give her an explanation

3.____

4. Charging out records until a specified due date, with prompt follow-up if they are not returned, is a
    A. *good* idea; it may prevent the records from being kept needlessly on someone's desk for long periods of time
    B. *good* idea; it will indicate the extent of your authority to other departments
    C. *poor* idea; the person borrowing the material may make an error because of the pressure put upon him to return the records
    D. *poor* idea; other departments will feel that you do not trust them with the records and they will be resentful

4._____

Questions 5-9.

DIRECTIONS: Questions 5 through 9 consist of three lines of code letters and numbers. The numbers on each line should correspond with the code letters on the same line in accordance with the table below.

Code Letter	P	L	I	J	B	O	H	U	C	G
Corresponding Letter	0	1	2	3	4	5	6	7	8	9

On some of the lines, an error exists in the coding. Compare the letters and numbers in each question carefully. If you find an error or errors on
  only one of the lines in the question, mark your answer A;
  any two lines in the question, mark your answer B;
  all three lines in the question, mark your answer C;
  none of the lines in the question, mark your answer D.

SAMPLE QUESTION
JHOILCP   3652180
BICLGUP   4286970
UCIBHLJ   5824613

In the above sample, the first line is correct since each code letter listed has the correct corresponding number. On the second line, an error exists because code letter L should have the number 1 instead of the number 6. On the third line, an error exists because the code letter U should have the number 7 instead of the number 5. Since there are errors on two of the three lines, the correct answer is B.

5. BULJCIP   4713920
    HIGPOUL   6290571
    OCUHJJBI   5876342

5._____

6. CUBLOIJ   8741023
    LCLGCLB   1818914
    JPUHIOC   3076158

6._____

7. OIJGCBPO   52398405
    UHPBLIOP   76041250
    CLUIPGPC   81720908

7._____

8. BPCOUOJI   40875732   8._____
    UOHCIPLB   75682014
    GLHUUCBJ   92677843

9. HOIOHJLH   65256361   9._____
    IOJJHHBP   25536640
    OJHBJOPI   53642502

Questions 10-13.

DIRECTIONS: Questions 10 through 13 are to be answered SOLELY on the basis of the information given in the following passage.

The mental attitude of the employee toward safety is exceedingly important in preventing accidents. All efforts designed to keep safety on the employee's mind and to keep accident prevention a live subject in the office will help substantially in a safety program. Although it may seem strange, it is common for people to be careless. Therefore, safety education is a continuous process.

Safety rules should be explained, and the reasons for their rigid enforcement should be given to employees. Telling employees to be careful or giving similar general safety warnings and slogans is probably of little value. Employees should be informed of basic safety fundamentals. This can be done through staff meetings, informal suggestions to employees, movies, and safety instruction cards. Safety instruction cards provide the employees with specific suggestions about safety and serve as a series of timely reminder helping to keep safety on the minds of employees. Pictures, posters, and cartoon sketches on bulletin boards that are located in areas continually used by employees arouse the employees' interest in safety. It is usually good to supplement this type of safety promotion with intensive individual follow-up.

10. The above passage implies that the LEAST effective of the following safety   10._____
    measures is
       A. rigid enforcement of safety rules
       B. getting employees to think in terms of safety
       C. elimination of unsafe conditions in the office
       D. telling employees to stay alert at all times

11. The reason given by the passage for maintaining ongoing safety education is   11._____
    that
       A. people are often careless
       B. office tasks are often dangerous
       C. the value of safety slogans increases with repetition
       D. safety rules change frequently

12. Which one of the following safety aids is MOST likely to be preferred by the   12._____
    passage? A
       A. cartoon of a man tripping over a carton and yelling, *Keep aisles clear!*
       B. poster with a large number one and a caption saying, *Safety First*

C. photograph of a very neatly arranged office
D. large sign with the word THINK in capital letters

13. Of the following, the BEST title for the above passage is   13.____
    A. Basic Safety Fundamentals
    B. Enforcing Safety Among Careless Employees
    C. Attitudes Toward Safety
    D. Making Employees Aware of Safety

Questions 14-21.

DIRECTIONS: Questions 14 through 21 are to be answered SOLELY on the basis of the information and chart given below.

The following chart shows expenses in five selected categories for a one-year period, expressed as percentages of these same expenses during the previous year. The chart compares two different offices. In Office T (represented by ▓▓▓▓), a cost reduction program has been tested for the past year. The other office, Office Q (represented by ////), served as a control, in that no special effort was made to reduce costs during the past year.

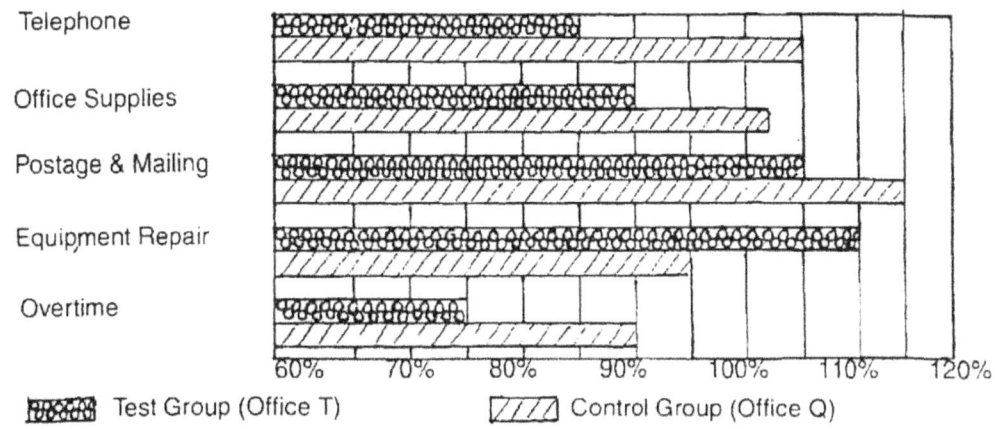

14. In Office T, which category of expense showed the greatest percentage   14.____
    REDUCTION from 2019 to 2020?
    A. Telephone   B. Office Supplies
    C. Postage & Mailing   D. Overtime

15. In which expense category did Office T show the BEST results in percentage   15.____
    terms when compared to Office Q?
    A. Telephone   B. Office Supplies
    C. Postage & Mailing   D. Overtime

16. According to the above chart, the cost reduction program was LEAST effective for the expense category of
    A. Office Supplies
    B. Postage & Mailing
    C. Equipment Repair
    D. Overtime

17. Office T's telephone costs went down during 2020 by approximately how many percentage points?
    A. 15
    B. 20
    C. 85
    D. 104

18. Which of the following changes occurred in expenses for Office Supplies in Office Q in the year 2020 as compared with the year 2019?
    They
    A. increased by more than 100%
    B. remained the same
    C. decreased by a few percentage points
    D. increased by a few percentage points

19. For which of the following expense categories do the results in Office T and the results in Office Q differ MOST NEARLYY by 10 percentage points?
    A. Telephone
    B. Postage & Mailing
    C. Equipment Repair
    D. Overtime

20. In which expense category did Office Q's costs show the GREATEST percentage increase in 2020?
    A. Telephone
    B. Office Supplies
    C. Postage & Mailing
    D. Equipment Repair

21. In Office T, by approximately what percentage did overtime expense change during the past year? It
    A. *increased* by 15%
    B. *increased* by 75%
    C. *decreased* by 10%
    D. *decreased* by 25%

22. In a particular agency, there were 160 accidents in 2017. Of these accidents, 75% were due to unsafe acts and the rest were due to unsafe conditions. In the following year, a special safety program was established. The number of accidents in 2019 due to unsafe acts was reduced to 35% of what it had been in 2017.
    How many accidents due to unsafe acts were there in 2019?
    A. 20
    B. 36
    C. 42
    D. 56

23. At the end of every month, the petty cash fund of Agency A is reimbursed for payments made from the fund during the month. During the month of February, the amounts paid from the fund were entered on receipts as follows: 10 bus fares of $3.50 each and one taxi fare of $35.00. At the end of the month, the money left in the fund was in the following denominations: 15 ten-dollar bills, 10 one-dollar bills, 40 quarters, and 100 dimes.
    If the petty cash fund is reduced by 20% for the following month, how much money will there be available in the petty cash fund for March?
    A. $110.00
    B. $200.00
    C. $215.00
    D. $250.00

24. The one of the following records which it would be MOST advisable to keep in alphabetical order is a
    A. continuous listing of phone messages, including time and caller, for your supervisor
    B. listing of individuals currently employed by your agency in a particular title
    C. record of purchases paid for by the petty cash fund
    D. dated record of employees who have borrowed material from the files in your office

25. Assume that you have been asked to copy by hand a column of numbers with two decimal places from one record to another. Each number consists of three, four, and five digits.
    In order to copy them quickly and accurately, you should copy
    A. each number exactly, making sure that the column of digits farthest to the right is in a straight line and all other columns are lined up
    B. the column of digits farthest to the right and then copy the next column of digits moving from right to left
    C. the column of digits farthest to the left and then copy the next column of digits moving from left to right
    D. the digits to the right of each decimal point and then copy the digits to the left of each decimal point

KEY (CORRECT ANSWERS)

1.	D		11.	A
2.	A		12.	A
3.	D		13.	D
4.	A		14.	D
5.	A		15.	A
6.	C		16.	C
7.	D		17.	A
8.	B		18.	D
9.	C		19.	B
10.	D		20.	C

21. D
22. C
23. B
24. B
25. A

READING COMPREHENSION
UNDERSTANDING AND INTERPRETING WRITTEN MATERIAL
EXAMINATION SECTION
TEST 1

DIRECTIONS: All questions are to be answered SOLELY on the basis of the information contained in the passage. Each question or incomplete statement is followed by several suggested answers or completions. Select the one that BEST answers the question or completes the statement. *PRINT THE LETTER OF THE CORRECT ANSWER IN THE SPACE AT THE RIGHT.*

Questions 1-3.

The equipment in a mail room may include a mail-metering machine. This machine simultaneously stamps, postmarks, seals, and counts letters as fast as the operator can feed them. It can also print the proper postage directly on a gummed strip to be affixed to bulky items. It is equipped with a meter which is removed from the machine and sent to the postmaster to be set for a given number of stampings of any denomination. The setting of the meter must be paid for in advance. One of the advantages of metered mail is that it bypasses the cancellation operation and, thereby, facilitates handling by the post office. Mail metering also makes the pilfering of stamps impossible, but does not prevent the passage of personal mail in company envelopes through the meters unless there is established a rigid control or censorship over outgoing mail.

1. According to this statement, the postmaster 1.____
   A. is responsible for training new clerks in the use of mail-metering machines
   B. usually recommends that both large and small firms adopt the use of mail metering machines
   C. is responsible for setting the meter to print a fixed number of stampings
   D. examines the mail-metering machines to see that they are properly installed in the mail room

2. According to this statement, the use of mail-metering machines 2.____
   A. requires the employment of more clerks in a mail room than does the use of postage stamps
   B. interferes with the handling of large quantities of outgoing mail
   C. does not prevent employees from sending their personal letters at company expense
   D. usually involves smaller expenditures for mail room equipment than does the use of postage stamps

3. On the basis of this statement, it is MOST accurate to state that 3.____
   A. mail-metering machines are often used for opening envelopes
   B. postage stamps are generally used when bulky packages are to be mailed
   C. the use of metered mail tends to interfere with rapid mail handling by the post office
   D. mail-metering machines can seal and count letters at the same time

Questions 4-8.

It is the Housing Administration's policy that all tenants, whether new or transferring from one housing development to another, shall be required to pay a standard security deposit of one month's rent based on the rent at the time of admission. There are, however, certain exceptions to this policy. Employees of the Administration shall not be required to pay a security deposit if they secure an apartment in an Administration development. Where the payment of a full security deposit may present a hardship to a tenant, the development's manager may allow a tenant to move into an apartment upon payment of only part of the security deposit. In such cases, however, the tenant must agree to gradually pay the balance of the deposit. If a tenant transfers from one apartment to another within the same project, the security deposit originally paid by the tenant for his former apartment will be acceptable for his new apartment, even if the rent in the new apartment is greater than the rent in the former one. Finally, tenants who receive public assistance need not pay a security deposit before moving into an apartment if the appropriate agency states, in writing, that it will pay the deposit. However, it is the responsibility of the development's manager to make certain that payment shall be received within one month of the date the tenant moves into the apartment.

4. According to the above passage, when a tenant transfers from one apartment to another in the same development, the Housing Administration will
   A. accept the tenant's old security deposit as the security deposit for his new apartment
   B. refund the tenant's old security deposit and not require him to pay a new deposit
   C. keep the tenant's old security deposit and require him to pay a new deposit
   D. require the tenant to pay a new security deposit based on the difference between his old rent and his new rent

5. On the basis of the above passage, it is INCORREC to state that a tenant who receives public assistance may move into an Administration development if
   A. he pays the appropriate security deposit
   B. the appropriate agency gives a written indication that it will pay the security deposit before the tenant moves in
   C. the appropriate agency states, by telephone, that it will pay the security deposit
   D. the appropriate agency writes the manager to indicate that the security deposit will be paid within one month but not less than two weeks from the date the tenant moves into the apartment

6. On the basis of the above passage, a tenant who transfers from an apartment in one development to an apartment in a different department will
   A. forfeit his old security deposit and be required to pay another deposit
   B. have his old security deposit refunded and not have to pay a new deposit
   C. pay the difference between his old security deposit and the new one
   D. have to pay a security deposit based on the new apartment's rent

7. The Housing Administration will NOT require payment of a security deposit if a tenant
   A. is an Administration employee
   B. is receiving public assistance
   C. claims that payment will present a hardship
   D. indicates, in writing, that he will be responsible for any damage done to his apartment

8. Of the following, the BEST title for the above passage is:
   A. Security Deposits – Transfers
   B. Security Deposits – Policy
   C. Exemptions and Exceptions – Security Deposits
   D. Amounts – Security Deposits

Questions 9-11.

Terrazzo flooring will last a very long time if it is cared for properly. Lacquers, shellac or varnish preparations should never be used on terrazzo. Soap cleaners are not recommended, since they dull the appearance of the floor. Alkaline solutions are harmful, so neutral cleaner or non-alkaline synthetic detergents will give best results. If the floor is very dirty, it may be necessary to scrub it. The same neutral cleaning solution should be used for scrubbing as for mopping. Scouring powder may be sprinkled at particularly dirty spots. Do not use steel wool for scrubbing. Small pieces of steel filings left on the floor will rust and discolor the terrazzo. Non-woven nylon or open-mesh fabric abrasive pads are suitable for scrubbing terrazzo floors.

9. According to the above passage, the BEST cleaning agent for terrazzo flooring is a(n)
   A. soap cleaner   B. varnish preparation
   C. neutral cleaner   D. alkaline solution

10. According to the above passage, terrazzo floors should NOT be scrubbed with
    A. non-woven nylon abrasive pads   B. steel wool
    C. open-mesh fabric abrasive pads D. scouring powder

11. As used in the above passage, the word *discolor* means MOST NEARLY
    A. crack   B. scratch   C. dissolve   D. stain

Questions 12-15.

Planning for the unloading of incoming trucks is not easy since generally little or no advance notice of truck arrivals is received. The height of the floor of truck bodies and loading platforms sometimes are different; this makes necessary the use of special unloading methods. When available, hydraulic ramps compensate for the differences in platform and truck floor levels. When hydraulic ramps are not available, forklift equipment can sometimes be used, if the truck sprigs are strong enough to support such equipment. In a situation like this, the unloading operation does not differ much from unloading a railroad box car in the cases where the forklift truck or a hydraulic pallet jack cannot be used inside the truck, a pallet dolly should be placed inside the truck, so that the empty pallet can be loaded close to the truck contents and rolled easily to the truck door and platform.

12. According to the above passage, unloading trucks are
    A. easy to plan since the time of arrival is usually known beforehand
    B. the same as loading a railroad box car
    C. hard to plan since trucks arrive without notice
    D. a very normal thing to do

13. According to the above passage, which materials-handling equipment can make up for the difference in platform and truck floor levels?
    A. Hydraulic jacks
    B. Hydraulic ramps
    C. Forklift trucks
    D. Conveyors

14. According to the above passage, what materials-handling equipment can be used when a truck cannot support the weight of forklift equipment?
    A. A pallet dolly
    B. A hydraulic ramp
    C. Bridge plates
    D. A warehouse tractor

15. Which of the following is the BEST title for the above passage?
    A. Unloading Railroad Box Cars
    B. Unloading Motor Trucks
    C. Loading Rail Box
    D. Loading Motor Trucks

Questions 16-19.

Ventilation, as used in firefighting operations, means opening up a building or structure in which a fire is burning to release the accumulated heat, smoke, and gases. Lack of knowledge of the principle of ventilation on the part of firemen may result in unnecessary punishment due to ventilation being neglected or improperly handled. While ventilation itself extinguishes no fires, when used in an intelligent manner, it allows firemen to get at the fire more quickly, easily, and with less danger and hardship.

16. According to the above passage, the MOST important result of failure to apply the principles of ventilation at a fire may be
    A. loss of public confidence
    B. disciplinary action
    C. waste of water
    D. excessive use of equipment
    E. injury to fireman

17. It may be inferred from the above passage that the CHIEF advantage of ventilation is that it
    A. eliminates the need for gas masks
    B. reduces smoke damage
    C. permits firemen to work closer to the fire
    D. cools the fire
    E. enables firemen to use shorter hose lines

18. Knowledge of the principles of ventilation, as defined in the above passage, would be LEAST important in a fire in a
    A. tenement house
    B. grocery store
    C. ship's hold
    D. lumberyard
    E. office building

5 (#1)

19. We may conclude from the above passage that, for the well-trained and equipped fireman, ventilation is 19._____
    A. a simple matter
    B. rarely necessary
    C. relatively unimportant
    D. a basic tool
    E. sometimes a handicap

Questions 20-22.

Many public service and industrial organizations are becoming increasingly insistent that supervisors at the work level be qualified instructors. The reason for this is that technological improvements and overall organizational growth require the acquisition of new skills and knowledge by workers. These skills and knowledge can be acquired in two ways. They can be gained either by absorption-rubbing shoulders with the job or through planned instruction. Permitting the acquisition of new skills and knowledge is to be haphazard and uncertain is too costly. At higher supervisory levels, the need for instructing subordinate is not so obvious, but it is just as important as at the lowest work level. A high-ranking supervisor accomplishes the requirements of his position only if his subordinate supervisors perform their work efficiently. Regardless of one's supervisory position, the ability to instruct easily and efficiently helps to insure well-qualified and thoroughly-trained subordinates. There exists an unfounded but rather prevalent belief that becoming a competent instructor is a long, arduous, and complicated process. This belief arises partially as a result of the requirement of a long period of college preparation involved in preparing teachers for our school system. This time is necessary because teachers must learn a great deal of subject matter. The worker who advances to a supervisory position generally has superior skill and knowledge; therefore, he has only to learn the techniques by which he can impart his knowledge in order to become a competent instructor.

20. According to the above passage, a prolonged period of preparation for instructing is NOT generally necessary for a worker who is advanced to a supervisory position because 20._____
    A. he may already possess some of the requirements of a competent instructor
    B. his previous job knowledge is generally sufficient to enable him to begin instructing immediately
    C. in his present position there is less need for the specific job knowledge of the ordinary worker
    D. the ability to instruct follows naturally from superior skill and knowledge

21. According to the above passage, it is important for the higher-level supervisor to be a good instructor because 21._____
    A. at this level there is a tendency to overlook the need for instruction of both subordinate supervisors and workers
    B. good training practices will then be readily adopted by lower-level supervisors
    C. the need for effective training is more critical at the higher levels of responsibility
    D. training can be used to improve the supervisory performance of his subordinate supervisors

22. According to the above passage, the acquisition of new skills and knowledge by workers is BEST accomplished when
    A. the method of training allows for the use of absorption
    B. organizational growth and technological improvement indicate a need for further training
    C. such training is the result of careful planning
    D. the cost factor involved in training can be readily justified

Questions 23-25.

The organization of any large agency falls into three broad general zones: top management, middle management, and rank-and-file operations. The normal task of middle management is to supervise, direct, and control the performance of operations within the scope of law, policy, and regulations already established. Where policy is settled and well defined, middle management is basically a set of standard operations, although they may call for high-developed skills. Where, however, policy is not clearly stated, is ambiguous, or is rapidly shifting, middle management is likely to have an important influence upon emergency policy trends. Persons working in the zone of middle management usually become specialists. They need specialist knowledge of law, rules, and regulations, and court decisions governing their organization if they are to discharge their duties effectively. They will also have acquired specialist knowledge of relationships and sequences in the normal flow of business. Further, their attention is brought to bear on a particular administrative task, in a particular jurisdiction, with a particular clientele. The importance of middle management is obviously great. The reasons for such importance are not difficult to find: Here it is that the essential action of government in behalf of citizens is taken; here it is that citizens deal with government when they pass beyond their first contacts; here is a training ground from which a considerable part of top management emerges; and here it is that the spirit and temper of the public service and its reputation are largely made.

23. According to the above passage, the critical importance of middle management is due to the fact that it is at this level that
    A. formal executive training can be most useful
    B. the greatest amount of action is taken on the complaints of the general public
    C. the official actions taken have the greatest impact on general attitudes towards the public service
    D. the public most frequently comes in contact with governmental operations and agencies

24. According to the above passage, the one of the following statements which is NOT offered as an explanation of the tendency for middle management responsibility to produce specialists is that
    A. middle-management personnel frequently feel that their work is the most important in an organization
    B. specialized knowledge is acquired during the course of everyday work
    C. specialized knowledge is necessary for effective job performance
    D. their work assignments are directed to specific problems in specific situations

25. According to the above passage, the GREATEST impact of middle management in policy determination would be likely to be felt in the situation in which
    A. middle management possesses highly developed operational skills
    B. several policy directives from top management are subject to varying interpretations
    C. the authority of middle management to supervise, direct, and control operations has been clearly established
    D. top management has neglected to consider the policy views of middle management

KEY (CORRECT ANSWERS)

1.	C	11.	D
2.	C	12.	C
3.	D	13.	B
4.	A	14.	A
5.	C	15.	B
6.	D	16.	E
7.	A	17.	C
8.	B	18.	D
9.	C	19.	D
10.	B	20.	A

21.	D
22.	C
23.	C
24.	A
25.	B

TEST 2

DIRECTIONS: All questions are to be answered SOLELY on the basis of the information contained in the passage. Each question or incomplete statement is followed by several suggested answers or completions. Select the one that BEST answers the question or completes the statement. *PRINT THE LETTER OF THE CORRECT ANSWER IN THE SPACE AT THE RIGHT.*

Questions 1-2.

Metal spraying is used for many purposes. Worn bearings on shafts and spindles can be readily restored to original dimensions with any desired metal or alloy. Low-carbon steel shafts may be supplied with high-carbon steel journal surfaces, which can then be ground to size after spraying. By using babbitt wire, bearings can be lined or babbited while rotating. Pump shafts and impellers can be coated with any desired metal to overcome wear and corrosion. Valve seats may be re-surfaced. Defective castings can be repaired by filling in blowholes and checks. The application of metal spraying to the field of corrosion resistance is growing, although the major application in this field is in the use of sprayed zinc. Tin, lead, and aluminum have been used considerably. The process is used for structural and tank applications in the field as well as in the shop.

1. According to the above passage, worn bearing surface on shafts are metal-sprayed in order to
   A. prevent corrosion of the shaft
   B. fit them into larger-sized impellers
   C. returns them to their original sizes
   D. replaces worn babbitt metal

   1.____

2. According to the above passage, rotating bearings can be metal-sprayed using
   A. babbitt wire   B. high-carbon steel
   C. low-carbon steel   D. any desired metal

   2.____

Questions 3-5.

The method of cleaning which should generally be used is the space assignment method. Under this method, the buildings to be cleaned are divided into different sections. Within each section, each crew of Custodial Assistants is assigned to do one particular cleaning job. For example, within a section, one crew may be assigned to cleaning offices, another to scrubbing floors, a third to collecting trash, and so on. Other methods which may be used are the post-assignment methods and the gang-cleaning method. Under the post-assignment method, a Custodial Assistant is assigned to one area of a building and performs all cleaning jobs in that area. This method is seldom used except where buildings are so small and distant from each other that it is not economical to use the space-assigned method. Under the gang-cleaning method, a Custodial Foreman takes a number of Custodial Assistants through a section of the building. These Custodial Assistants work as a group and complete the various cleaning jobs as they go. This method is generally used only where the building contains very large open areas.

3. According to the above passage, under the space-assignment method, each crew generally
   A. works as a group and does a variety of different cleaning jobs
   B. is assigned to one area and performs all cleaning jobs in that area
   C. does one particular cleaning job within a section of a building
   D. follows the Custodial Foreman through a building containing large, open areas

4. According to the above passage, the post-assignment method is used mostly where the buildings to be cleaned are _____ in size and situated _____.
   A. large; close together
   B. small; close together
   C. large; far apart
   D. small; far apart

5. As used in the above passage, the word *economical* means MOST NEARLY
   A. thrifty   B. agreed   C. unusual   D. wasteful

Questions 6-9.

The desirability of complete refuse collection by municipalities is becoming generally accepted. In many cases, however, such ideal service is economically impractical and certain limits must be imposed. Some municipal authorities find it necessary to regulate the quantity of refuse, by weight or volume, which will be collected from a single residence or place of business at one collection. The purpose of the regulations is twofold: First, to maintain the degree of service rendered on a somewhat uniform basis; and, second, to insure a more or less constant collection from week to week. If left unregulated, careless producers might permit large quantities of refuse to accumulate on their premises over long periods and place abnormal amounts out for collection at irregular intervals, thus upsetting the collection schedule. Regulation is especially applied to large wholesale, industrial, and manufacturing enterprises which, in the great majority of cases, are required to dispose of all or part of their refuse themselves, at their own expense. The maximum quantities permitted by regulation should obviously be sufficient to take care of a normal accumulation at a household over the established interval between regular collections. In commercial districts, the maximum quantity limitations are often fixed on arbitrary bases rather than on normal production.

6. According to the above passage, many municipalities do not have complete refuse collections because
   A. it costs too much
   B. it is difficult to regulate
   C. it is not a municipal function
   D. they don't consider it desirable

7. According to the above passage, regulation by municipalities of the amount of refuse collected per collection from any one place of business does NOT contribute to
   A. accumulation of refuse by careless producers
   B. maintenance of collection schedules
   C. steady collection from one week to the next
   D. uniform service

8. According to the above passage, regulations by municipalities of refuse collection from certain enterprises helps to cut down
   A. accumulation of refuse for private collection
   B. the amount of refuse produced
   C. variation in the volume of refuse produced
   D. variation in collection service

8.____

9. According to the above passage, municipalities limit the amount of refuse collected in commercial districts on an arbitrary basis rather than on the basis of a normal accumulation. This is probably done because
   A. arbitrary standards are easy to establish and enforce
   B. normal accumulation is different for each district
   C. normal accumulation would require the collection of too much refuse
   D. there is no such thing as a normal accumulation

9.____

Questions 10-13.

The following passage is adapted from an old office manual:

Modern office methods, geared to ever higher speeds and aimed at ever greater efficiency, are largely the result of the typewriter. The typewriter is a substitute for handwriting and, in the hands of a skilled typist, not only turns out letters and other documents at least three times faster than a penman can do the work, but turns out the greater volume more uniformly and legibly. With the use of carbon paper and onionskin paper, identical copies can be made at the same time.

The typewriter, besides its effect on the conduct of business and government, has had a very important effect on the position of women. The typewriter has done much to bring women into business and government and today there are vastly more women than men typists. Many women have used the keys of the typewriter to climb the ladder to responsible managerial positions.

The typewriter, as its name implies, employs type to make an ink impression on paper. For many years, the manual typewriter was the standard machine used. Today, the electric typewriter is dominant, and completely automatic typewriters are coming into wider use.

The mechanism of the office manual typewriter includes a set of keys arranged systematically in rows; a semicircular frame of type, connected to the keys by levers; the carriage, or paper carrier; a rubber roller, called a platen, against which the type strikes; and an inked ribbon which makes the impression of the type character when the key strikes it.

10. The above passage mentions a number of good features of the combination of a skilled typist and a typewriter. Of the following, the feature which is NOT mentioned in the passage is
    A. speed   B. uniformity   C. reliability   D. legibility

10.____

11. According to the above passage, a skilled typist can
    A. turn out at least five carbon copies of typed matter
    B. type at least three times faster than a penman can write
    C. type more than 80 words a minute
    D. readily move into a managerial position

11.____

54

4 (#2)

12. According to the above passage, which of the following is NOT part of the mechanism of a manual typewriter? 12._____
    A. Carbon paper
    B. Paper carrier
    C. Platen
    D. Inked ribbon

13. According to the above passage, the typewriter has helped 13._____
    A. men more than women in business
    B. women in career advancement into management
    C. men and women equally, but women have taken better advantage of it
    D. more women than men, because men generally dislike routine typing work

Questions 14-18.

Reductions in pipe size of a building heating system are made with eccentric fittings and are pitched downward. The ends of mains with gravity return shall be at least 18" above the water line of the boiler. As condensate flows opposite to the steam, run outs are one size larger than the vertical pipe and are pitched upward. In a one-pipe system, an automatic air vent must be provided at each main to relieve air pressure and to let steam enter the radiator. As steam enters the radiator, a *thermal* device causes the vent to close, thereby holding the steam. Steam mains should not be less than two inches in diameter. The end of the steam main should have a minimum size of one-half of its greatest diameter. Small steam systems should be sized for a 2-oz. pressure drop. Large steam systems should be sized for a 4-oz. pressure drop.

14. The word *thermal*, as used in the above passage, means MOST NEARLY 14._____
    A. convector   B. heat   C. instrument   D. current

15. According to the above passage, the one of the following that is one size larger than the vertical pipe is the 15._____
    A. steam main   B. valve   C. water line   D. run out

16. According to the above paragraph, small steam systems should be sized for a pressure drop of _____ oz. 16._____
    A. 2   B. 3   C. 4   D. 5

17. According to the above passage, ends of mains with gravity return shall be AT LEAST 17._____
    A. 18" above the water line of the boiler
    B. one-quarter of the greatest diameter of the main
    C. twice the size of the vertical pipe in the main
    D. 18" above the steam line of the boiler

18. According to the above passage, the one of the following that is provided at each main to relieve air pressure is a(n) 18._____
    A. gravity return   B. convector   C. eccentric   D. vent

55

Questions 19-21.

The bearings of all electrical equipment should be subjected to careful inspection at scheduled periodic intervals in order to secure maximum life. The newer type of sleeve bearing requires very little attention since the oil does not become contaminated and oil leakage is negligible. Maintenance of the correct oil level is frequently the only upkeep required for years of service with this type of bearing.

19. According to the above passage, the MAIN reason for making periodic inspections of electrical equipment is to
    A. reduce waste of lubricants
    B. prevent injury to operators
    C. make equipment last longer
    D. keeps operators "on their toes"

19.____

20. According to the above passage, the bearings of electrical equipment should be inspected
    A. whenever the equipment isn't working properly
    B. whenever there is time for inspections
    C. at least once a year
    D. at regular times

20.____

21. According to the above passage, when using the newer type of sleeve bearings,
    A. oil leakage is slight
    B. the oil level should be checked every few years
    C. oil leakage is due to carelessness
    D. oil soon becomes dirty

21.____

Questions 22-25.

There is hardly a city in the country that is not short of fire protection in some areas within its boundaries. These municipalities have spread out and have re-shuffled their residential, business, and industrial districts without readjusting the existing protective fire forces; or creating new protection units. Fire stations are still situated according to the needs of earlier times and have not been altered or improved to house modern firefighting equipment. They are neither efficient for carrying out their tasks nor livable for the men who must occupy them.

22. Of the following, the title which BEST describes the central idea of the above passage is:
    A. The Dynamic Nature of Contemporary Society
    B. The Cost of Fire Protection
    C. The Location and Design of Fire Stations
    D. The Design and Use of Firefighting Equipment
    E. The Growth of American Cities

22.____

23. According to the above passage, fire protection is inadequate in the United Sates in
    A. most areas of some cities
    B. some areas of most cities
    C. some areas in all cities
    D. all areas in some cities
    E. most areas in most cities

23.____

6 (#2)

24. The one of the following criteria for planning of fire stations which is NOT mentioned in the above passage is:
  A. Comfort of Firemen
  B. Proper Location
  C. Design for Modern Equipment
  D. Efficiency of Operation
  E. Cost of Construction

24.____

25. Of the following suggestions for improving the fire service, the one which would BEST deal with the problem discussed in the above passage would involve
  A. specialized training in the use of modern fire apparatus
  B. replacement of obsolete fire apparatus
  C. revision of zoning laws
  D. longer basic training for probationary firemen
  E. reassignment of fire districts

25.____

Questions 26-30.

Stopping, standing, and parking of motor vehicles is regulated by law to keep the public highways open for a smooth flow of traffic, and to keep stopped vehicles from blocking intersections, driveways, signs, fire hydrants, and other areas that must be kept clear. These established regulations apply in all situations, unless otherwise indicated by signs. Other local restrictions are posted in the areas to which they apply. Three examples of these other types of restrictions, which may apply singly or in combination with one another are:
NO STOPPING: This means that a driver may not stop a vehicle for any purpose except when necessary to avoid interference with other vehicles, or in compliance with directions of a police officer or signal.
NO STANDING: This means that a driver may stop a vehicle only temporarily to actually receive or discharge passengers.
NO PARKING: This means that a driver may stop a vehicle only temporarily to actually load or unload merchandise or passengers. When stopped, it is advisable to turn on warning flashers, if equipped with them. However, one should never use a directional signal for this purpose, because it may confuse other drivers. Some NO PARKING signs prohibit parking between certain hours on certain days. For example, the sign may read NO PARKING 8 A.M. to 11 A.M., MONDAY, WEDNESDAY, FRIDAY. These signs are usually utilized on streets where cleaning operations take place on alternate days.

26. The parking regulation that applies to fire hydrants is an example of _____ regulations.
  A. local B. established C. posted D. temporary

26.____

27. When stopped in a NO PARKING zone, it is advisable to
  A. turn on the right directional signal to indicate to other drivers that you will remain stopped
  B. turn on the left directional signal to indicate to other drivers that you may be leaving the curb after a period of time
  C. turn on the warning flashers if your car is equipped with them
  D. put the vehicle in reverse so that the backup lights will be on to warn approaching cars that you have temporarily stopped

27.____

28. You may stop a vehicle temporarily to discharge passengers in an area under the restriction of a _____ zone.
    A. NO STOPPING – NO STANDING
    B. NO STANDING – NO PARKING
    C. NO PARKING – NO STOPPING
    D. NO STOPPING – NO STANDING – NO PARKING

29. A sign reads "NO PARKING 8 A.M. to 11 A.M., MONDAY, WEDNESDAY, FRIDAY."
    Based on this sign, an enforcement officer would issue a summons to a car that is parked on a
    A. Tuesday at 9:30 A.M.
    B. Wednesday at 12:00 A.M.
    C. Friday at 10:30 A.M.
    D. Saturday at 8:00 A.M.

30. NO PARKING signs prohibiting parking between certain hours, on certain days, are usually utilized on streets where
    A. vehicles frequently take on and discharge passengers
    B. cleaning operations take place on alternate days
    C. NO STOPPING signs have been ignored
    D. commercial vehicles take on and unload merchandise

KEY (CORRECT ANSWERS)

1.	C	11.	B	21.	A
2.	A	12.	A	22.	C
3.	C	13.	B	23.	B
4.	D	14.	B	24.	E
5.	A	15.	D	25.	E
6.	A	16.	A	26.	B
7.	A	17.	A	27.	C
8.	D	18.	D	28.	B
9.	C	19.	C	29.	C
10.	C	20.	D	30.	B

VERBAL & CLERICAL ABILITIES

PART I

DIRECTIONS: Compare each line of the COPY at the bottom of the page with the corresponding line of the ORIGINAL at the top. Each *word* or *abbreviation* or *digit* in the copy which is not exactly the same as in the original is ONE error. In each line, mark every word or abbreviation or figure that is wrong. Then count the errors you have marked in the line and enter the total number in the column at the right. The first line has been done correctly to show you just how to mark and where to enter the total number of errors in the line. Work quickly and accurately.

ORIGINAL

	Name	*Address*	*Amount*
1.	Dr. Jane Frazier	Madison, Ind.	$7385.96
2.	Mr. Michael Crane	Atlanta, Ga.	1435.64
3.	Dr. Frank Thompson	Troy, N. Y.	2537.96
4.	Miss Mary James	Washington, Conn.	4994.73
5.	Mrs. Sidney Mayo	Guilford, Maine	9734.52
6.	Prof. Hammond Taylor	Ann Arbor, Mich.	1320.49
7.	Mr. Francis Toddy	Chicopee, Mass.	2525.27
8.	Mrs. Sadie Miller	Denver, Colo.	8612.50
9.	Dr. Lysle Adams	Springfield, Ohio	5323.47
10.	Dean Penfield Revercomb	Hanover, N. H.	4096.54
11.	Prof. Guido Nervini	Daytona, Fla.	2651.92
12.	Mr. Joshua Schutte	Ogden, Utah	3074.91
13.	Mr. Laurence Rosenstein	Sharon, Pa.	1834.86
14.	Miss Margery Downing	Dover, N. J.	6223.48
15.	Prof. Russell Mueller	Pulaski, Va.	1473.32
16.	Mr. Bradford Gilchrist	Secaucus, N. J.	5294.30
17.	Mrs. Theresa Worchel	Bicknel, Ind.	3304.73
18.	Prof. Walter Flowerman	Munising, Mich.	1052.51
19.	Dr. Charles Witmer	Ridgway, Pa.	9652.78
20.	Mr. Clarence Osborn	Johnston, R. I.	2052.89

COPY

	Name	*Address*	*Amount*	*Number of Errors*
1.	~~Miss~~ Jane ~~Frasier~~	Madison, ~~Wis.~~	$73~~5~~8.96	5
2.	Dr. Michael Crane	Atalanta, Ga.	1434.54	
3.	Dr. Frank Thomson	Troy, N. J.	2538.96	
4.	Mrs. Marie Jones	Washington, Conn.	4884.73	
5.	Mrs. Sydney Mayo	Guilford, Maine	9734.52	
6.	Prof. Hammond Tayler	Anne Arbor, Mich.	1329.49	
7.	Mr. Frances Toddy	Chicopee, Mass.	2525.27	
8.	Mrs. Sady Muller	Denver, Col.	8612.50	
9.	Dr. Lysle Adams	Springfield, Mass.	5323.47	
10.	Dean Penfield Rivercomb	Hannover, N. H.	4096.53	
11.	Prof. Guido Nervini	Daytona, Fla.	2651.92	
12.	Mrs. Joshua Schute	Ogden, Wash.	3074.91	
13.	Dr. Laurance Rosenstein	Sharon, Pa.	1843.86	
14.	Miss Margary Downing	Dover, N. J.	6232.48	

2 (#1)

15.	Prof. Russell Mueller	Pulaski, Va.	1473.32	_____
16.	Dr. Bradford Gilcrist	Secacus, N. J.	5924.30	_____
17.	Mrs. Therese Worchel	Bucknel, Ind.	3304.73	_____
18.	Prof. Walter Flowerman	Munsing, Mich.	1052.51	_____
19.	Dr. Charles Witmer	Ridgeway, Pa.	9652.78	_____
20.	Mr. Clarence Osborn	Johnstown, R. I.	2052.89	_____

PART I

1.	5		11.	0
2.	4		12.	3
3.	3		13.	4
4.	4		14.	3
5.	1		15.	0
6.	3		16.	5
7.	1		17.	2
8.	3		18.	1
9.	1		19.	1
10.	3		20.	1

PART II

DIRECTION: After each name, write the number of the drawer in which that record should be fillede. Work quickly and accurately. The first two are marked correctly

1 Aa - Al	5 Bj - Br	9 Cp - Cz	13 Fa - Fr	17 Ha - Hz	21 Kp - Kz	25 Mj - Mo	29 Pa - Pr	33 Sa - Si	37 Tj - Tz
2 Am - Au	6 Bs - Bz	10 Da - Dz	14 Fs - Fz	18 Ia - Iz	22 La - Le	26 Mp - Mz	30 Ps - Pz	34 Sj - St	38 U - V
3 Av - Az	7 Ca - Ch	11 Ea - Er	15 Ga - Go	19 Ja - Jz	23 Lf - Lz	27 Na - Nz	31 Qa - Qz	35 Su - Sz	39 Wa - Wz
4 Ba - Bi	8 Ci - Co	12 Es - Ez	16 Gp - Gz	20 Ka - Ko	24 Ma - Mi	28 Oa - Oz	32 Ra - Rz	36 Ta - Ti	40 X - Y - Z

RECORDS

1. Kuczma, H. G.   21
2. Davidson, C.H.   10
3. Scranton, B.   ......
4. McBee, C. P.   ......
5. Borden, H. C.   ......
6. Kilsheimer, B. O. ......
7. Newman, F. D.   ......
8. Urban, A.   ......
9. Abt, E. A.   ......
10. Style, E.   ......
11. Clinton, C. N. ......
12. Ginn, F.   ......
13. Morse, F. W.   ......
14. Veach, T. B.   ......
15. Simon, M.   ......
16. Lowell, T. T.   ......
17. Fendt, A.   ......
18. Poll, F. W.   ......
22. Ruhalter, B.   ......
23. Luciano, K. M. ......
24. Scott, E. T.   ......
25. Janovic, A.   ......
26. Cabot, B. C. L. ......
27. Forrest, B. S. ......
28. Graves, P. S.   ......
29. Alan, S. C.   ......
30. Revere, P. D.   ......
31. Peksbury, P.   ......
32. Laurson, H.   ......
33. Bell, A. G.   ......
34. Crescent, P.   ......
35. Higgs, B. P.   ......
36. Weston, C. B.   ......
37. Conway, M.   ......
38. Shortlidge, L. L. ......
39. West, D. C.   ......
43. Washburn, S.   ......
44. Marquit, D. H. ......
45. Whittier, G.   ......
46. Brown, H. W.   ......
47. Erdely, S. P.   ......
48. Ansul, R. P.   ......
49. Harris, S. B.   ......
50. Nason, R. C.   ......
51. Kalter, R. V.   ......
52. Degener, L.   ......
53. Hughes, H. M.   ......
54. Gallon, M.   ......
55. Beatty, T.   ......
56. Gormac, H. B.   ......
57. Tarnay, S. C.   ......
58. Dyer, C. B.   ......
59. Sawtelle, P.B. ......
60. Metro, D. C.   ......

2 (#2)

19.	Yorkley, S. F.	40.	Tirdel, C. O.	61.	Quinn, R. S. ......
20.	Sperr, R.	41.	O'Regan, P. T.	62.	Tuttle, J. A. ......
21.	Baker, W.	42.	Ross, S. G.	63.	Rhees, L. ......

PART II

1.	21	16.	23	31.	29	46.	5	61.	31
2.	10	17.	13	32.	22	47.	11	62.	37
3.	33	18.	29	33.	4	48.	2	63.	32
4.	24	19.	40	34.	9	49.	17		
5.	5	20.	34	35.	17	50.	27		
6.	20	21.	4	36.	39	51.	20		
7.	27	22.	32	37.	8	52.	10		
8.	38	23.	23	38.	33	53.	17		
9.	1	24.	33	39.	39	54.	15		
10.	34	25.	19	40.	36	55.	4		
11.	8	26.	7	41.	28	56.	15		
12.	15	27.	13	42.	32	57.	36		
13.	25	28.	16	43.	39	58.	10		
14.	38	29.	1	44.	24	59.	33		
15.	33	30.	32	45.	39	60.	24		

PART III

DIRECTION: Solve these problems as quickly as you can. When you have finished each problem, write the answer in the space at the right. The sample is done correctly.

sample ___11___

sample	(1)	(2)	(3)	(4)	
6 +5 11	54 27 +5	97 -48	$9\overline{)2736}$	$\dfrac{3}{8}+\dfrac{1}{2}=$	(1) _____ (2) _____ (3) _____ (4) _____
(5)	(6)	(7)	(8)		(5) _____ (6) _____
$1/2 \times 1/2 =$	$1.50 ×5	596 ×27	1246 ×.4		(7) _____ (8) _____
(9)	(10)	(11)	(12)		(9) _____ (10) _____
$57.23 - 2.9 =$	352.4 979.5 43.2 +17.7	6657732 -4986941	3478 ×918		(11) _____ (12) _____
(13)	(14)	(15)	(16)		(13) _____ (14) _____
$27\overline{)15120}$	324.9 ×4.26	$7/8 \div 1\ 3/4 =$	$275 less 20%		(15) _____ (16) _____
(17)	(18)	(19)	(20)		(17) _____ (18) _____
$(3)^3 =$	24% of 546 =	$364\sqrt{4975.88}$	$\sqrt{20736}$		(19) _____ (20) _____

2 (#3)

PART III

1. 86
2. 49
3. 304
4. 7/8
5. 1/4

6. $7.50
7. 16,092
8. 498,4
9. 54.33
10. 1392.8

11. 1,670,791
12. 3,192,804
13. 560
14. 1384.074
15. 1/2

16. 220
17. 27
18. 131.04
19. 13.67
20. 144

PART IV

DIRECTIONS: Each of these tables contains ONE - and ONLY one - wrong number. To find the wrong number, first add the columns until you find one which does not add correctly, and then add accross until you find a row that adds wrong. At the intersection of these two (that is, where the incorrect row and the incorrect column cross or meet), is the ONE wrong number—mark it with an X. Any one of the numbers or totals may be wrong. The samples at the right are done correctly.

	Sample		Total
2	7	9	18
8	5	X	17
6	3	1	10
Total 16	15	14	45

	Sample		Total
5	7	9	21
12	4	3	19
2	6	1	9
Total 19	X	13	49

BEGIN HERE

(1)
			Total
1	6	8	10
2	9	6	17
2	3	1	6
Total 5	13	13	33

(2)
			Total
8	7	2	17
5	1	6	15
7	6	6	19
23	14	14	51

(3)
			Total
5	6	9	20
2	3	6	11
7	8	8	24
14	17	24	55

(4)
			Total
7	6	3	16
8	4	19	31
11	13	9	33
26	23	31	80

(5)
4	2	7	13
0	2	1	3
2	4	6	12
Total 8	8	14	28

(6)
2	8	8	18
2	5	8	15
5	8	4	18
10	21	20	51

(7)
7	3	6	16
5	12	8	23
9	9	8	26
21	34	22	67

(8)
9	6	9	24
0	18	12	40
7	7	36	50
16	31	57	104

(9)
3	6	0	9
9	6	3	18
0	7	2	9
Total 12	19	6	36

(10)
8	4	3	14
5	9	8	22
5	4	3	12
18	17	14	48

(11)
6	8	4	18
4	9	6	19
6	9	4	18
16	25	14	55

(12)
14	18	8	40
24	9	35	69
21	33	12	66
59	60	56	175

(13)
6	4	1	10
7	9	4	20
8	9	9	26
Total 21	22	14	57

(14)
6	8	0	16
6	3	3	12
8	7	2	17
22	18	5	45

(15)
12	9	6	27
4	12	8	24
3	5	21	27
19	26	35	80

(16)
10	24	16	50
36	16	48	102
12	36	21	69
58	78	85	221

(17)
4	7	7	18
5	6	5	16
2	9	6	17
Total 13	22	18	51

(18)
4	4	6	16
5	4	3	12
9	6	8	23
18	14	17	49

(19)
4	14	6	24
5	4	13	21
19	16	8	43
28	33	27	88

(20)
17	22	17	56
18	23	24	65
15	14	22	51
50	59	64	172

2 (#4)

PART IV

1.	6	11.	9
2.	5	12.	35
3.	8	13.	10
4.	5	14.	6
5.	8	15.	27
6.	5	16.	16
7.	34	17.	13
8.	0	18.	16
9.	6	19.	4
10.	48	20.	64

PART V

DIRECTIONS: Write the answer to each problem on the line at the right. Work quickly and accurately.

1. What is the total cost of two bottles of ink at $.10 a bottle and one dozen pencils at $.40 a dozen?

2. If peaches are selling at $.40 a can or $4.60 per dozen cans, how much is saved on each can by purchasing the dozen cans?

3. One room has 9 rows of filing cabinets with 9 filing cabinets in each row. Another room has 6 rows of cabinets with twelve cabinets in each row. How many more cabinets are there in the first room?

4. Ink sells at $.75 a quart. How much will 5 gallons cost?

5. The average cost per pound of sugar, tea, and coffee is $.30. If sugar costs $.10 and tea costs $.45, how much does coffee cost?

6. How many notebooks can be bought for $3.00 at the rate of 2 for $.50?

7. At 8 a.m. the barometric pressure was 30.6 and at 11 a.m. the pressure was 31.8. Assuming a constant rate of increase, what time was it when the pressure was 31.0?

8. A man earned $28 and saved $7. What percent of his earnings did he save?

9. The premium for $1000 of insurance is $50.00. What is the premium for $5500 of insurance?

10. A man worked one week from 9:00 to 4:00 with 30 minutes for lunch, and Saturday 9:00 to 1:00. How many hours did he work that week?

11. One dealer offers 25% discount on a $100 desk. Another offers successive discounts of 20% and 10% on the same desk. What is the difference between the net prices?

12. An employee received $400.00 for a 40 hour week. For time worked over this 40 hours he was paid at the rate of 1 1/2 times his regular hourly rate. How much will he receive when he works 52 hours in one week?

13. If a married man makes $24,000 a year and he can deduct $1500 personal exemption and $200 for various contributions and taxes, how much does he pay if the balance is taxed at the rate of 5%?

14. A wholesaler sold 1/3 of his supply of coal to one dealer, 1/4 of it to another, and the remainder at $16 a ton for $8000. How many tons of coal did he have in the first place?

15. If a piece rate operator earns 2/3 of a cent per sleeve facing and she gets rate and a half for every one over 2400 per week, what is her wage the week she makes $3100?

16. During his sixth year with the company an employee made $25,000 which is twice as much as he was paid during the first year. If his wage increased an equal amount each year, what was his salary the fourth year?

PART V

1. $.60
2. $.20
3. 9
4. $15
5. $.35
6. 12
7. 9 AM
8. 25%
9. $275
10. 36.5 hours
11. $3
12. $580
13. $1,115
14. 1200 tons
15. $23
16. $19,400

PART VI

DIRECTIONS: Some of the words below are correctly spelled and some are not. Where the spelling is WRONG, write the correct spelling in the space following the word. Do nothing when a word is spelled correctly. Work quickly.

1. already ....
2. goverment ....
3. accidant ....
4. deside ....
5. accept ....
6. committe ....
7. bussiness ....
8. minute ....
9. realy ....
10. invoise ....
11. consideration ....
12. assure ....
13. foriegn ....
14. responsability ....
15. application ....
16. develope ....
17. issue. ....
18. receive. ....
19. agreement ....
20. arrangment ....
21. experiance ....
22. charactor ....
23. organization ....
24. atheletic. ....
25. practical ....
26. convenient ....
27. referance ....
28. fourty ....
29. nuisence ....
30. beleive ....
31. guaranteed ....
32. definitly ....
33. ninth ....
34. permenent ....
35. apologize ....
36. remittance ....
37. immediatly ....
38. morgage ....
39. bookeeping ....
40. desireable ....
41. withhold ....
42. recomend ....
43. acknowlege ....
44. aquainted ....
45. proceed ....
46. ledger ....
47. hastely. ....
48. adjust. ....
49. interupt ....
50. equipped ....

PART VI

1. (correct)
2. government
3. accident
4. decide
5. (correct)//
6. committee
7. business
8. (correct)
9. really
10. invoice//
11. (correct)
12. (correct)
13. foreign
14. responsibility
15. (correct)//
16. develop
17. (correct)
18. (correct)
19. (correct)
20. arrangement//
21. experience
22. character
23. (correct)
24. athletic
25. (correct)//
26. (correct)
27. reference
28. forty
29. nuisance
30. believe//
31. (correct)
32. definitely
33. (correct)
34. permanent
35. (correct)//
36. (correct)
37. immediately
38. mortgage
39. bookkeeping
40. desirable//
41. (correct)
42. recommend
43. acknowledge
44. acquainted
45. (correct)//
46. (correct)
47. hastily
48. (correct)
49. interrupt
50. (correct)

PART VII

DIRECTIONS: Read each paragraph and the statements following it. On the line at the right put the number of the word or phrase which best completes the statement or answers the question. Work quickly and accurately.

The Unfair Trade Practices Act (law in Kansas) follows closely the model bill of the National Food and Grocery Conference Committee and requires:(1) that a wholesaler must add a markup of at least two percent to the cost of his merchandise; (2) that a retailer must add a markup of at least six percent to the cost of his merchandise; (3) that the cost to the retailer must include cartage from the wholesaler or warehouse which is presumed to be three-fourths of one percent in the absence of proof to the contrary.

1. The Act requires that a wholesaler must:(1) add a 2% markup to the selling price; (2) add a 6% markup to merchandise cost; (3) add a 2% markup to all groceries; (4) add a mark-up of 2c/o to merchandise cost

2. The cost to the retailer must include: (1) cartage from the wholesaler or the warehouse; (2) cartage from the wholesaler or warehouse of one percent; (3) allowance for whole-sale cartage of one quarter of one percent; (4) cartage allowance of three percent

3. The Kansas Unfair Trade Practices Act and the National Food and Grocery Conference Committee Bill are: (1) the same; (2) very different; (3) very similar; (4) contradictory

4. The cartage costs are always assumed to be three-fourths of one percent: (1) in the absence of contrary evidence; (2) unless the retailer states otherwise; (3) unless the consumer objects; (4) unless they are 1%

5. The Act: (1) became law many years ago; (2) was passed by Congress; (3) became law in Kansas; (4) failed to pass in Kansas

6. The markup required of the retailer is: (1) the same as that required of the wholesaler; (2) is more than that required of the wholesaler; (3) is less than that required of the wholesaler; (4) is left to the Conference Committee to determine

7. The Law is concerned with: (1) the amount the merchant can pay for cartage; (2) the kinds of merchandise he can sell; (3) the number of retailers served by a wholesaler; (4) the prices which merchants must charge

Requisition of Supplies and Service

Office supplies regularly stocked consist of such frequently used items as pencils, paper clips, rubber bands, copy paper, typewriter ribbons, etc. These may be obtained, as needed, by telephoning Mr. Jones and requesting delivery of desired quantity. Monthly statements of stock used by each department will be sent to Department Head for record. Pink order forms should be used for ordering printed material (bills, letterheads, etc.). These should be sent to Mr. Jones via interoffice mail. If repair service is needed for office machines, call Miss Crosby and give her the details (type of machine, difficulty, when needed). When repairs have been made, inform her of this fact so that charges may be approved for payment. When it is necessary to order special items not carried in stock, comparative estimates of cost must be obtained and item ordered from lowest bidder on blue order form, approved by both Department Head and Auditor.

8. A written order is necessary to obtain: (1) all supplies; (2) typewriter repairs; (3) letterheads; (4) pencils

9. Orders for copy machine repairs will be handled by: (1) Department Head; (2) Mr. Jones; (3) stockroom; (4) Miss Crosby

10. On which orders is the Auditor's approval necessary? (1) pink; (2) blue; (3) repairs; (4) stockroom

11. Printed forms are ordered from: (1) Mr. Jones; (2) Miss Crosby; (3) Auditor; (4) printer....

12. Comparative bids should be obtained before ordering: (1) special equipment; (2) repairs; (3) printed forms; (4) carbon paper

13. Charges for repairs are approved for payment by: (1) Mr. Jones; (2) Department Head; (3) Auditor; (4) Miss Crosby

14. Monthly statements will be sent covering: (1) all supplies used; (2) supplies ordered from stock; (3) repair service; (4) supplies and repairs

---

PART VII

1. 4
2. 1
3. 3
4. 1
5. 3
6. 2
7. 4
8. 3
9. 4
10. 2
11. 1
12. 1
13. 4
14. 1

PART VIII

DIRECTIONS: On the line at the right write the NUMBER of the word which means most nearly the same as the word in capitals. The first one has been done correctly. Work quickly and accurately.

	NEGLECT	(1) disregard	(2) respond	(3) record	(4) indication
1.	INVESTIGATION	(1) inquiry	(2) data	(3) punishment	(4) imitation
2.	SELECT	(1) inherit	(2) release	(3) choose	(4) conform
3.	PROHIBIT	(1) prevail	(2) command	(3) forbid	(4) annoy
4.	LOATHE	(1) bristle	(2) detest	(3) abstain	(4) relish
5.	ACCURATE	(1) valuable	(2) exact	(3) careless	(4) perceptive
6.	MINIMUM	(1) oldest	(2) best	(3) pleasant	(4) least
7.	ANONYMOUS	(1) famous	(2) autonomous	(3) suspicious	(4) nameless
8.	PROCEDURE	(1) method	(2) precedence	(3) production	(4) acquittal
9.	DEPORTATION	(1) banishment	(2) immigration	(3) potation	(4) derangement
10.	ACCUMULATE	(1) amass	(2) enforce	(3) disburse	(4) consign
11.	MEAGER	(1) negative	(2) abundant	(3) fierce	(4) scant
12.	COMPETENT	(1) congenial	(2) qualified	(3) sluggish	(4) instructive
13.	TERMINATE	(1) consign	(2) hinder	(3) agree	(4) conclude
14.	ABOLISH	(1) denounce	(2) end	(3) admonish	(4) renounce
15.	COMPUTE	(1) create	(2) credit	(3) commence	(4) calculate
16.	PREJUDICE	(1) opponent	(2) caution	(3) anger	(4) bias
17.	DILIGENT	(1) industrious	(2) ambitious	(3) honest	(4) wise
18.	OMNIPOTENT	(1) merciful	(2) almighty	(3) powerless	(4) righteous
19.	FURTIVE	(1) stealthy	(2) overt	(3) furry	(4) wanton
20.	OBSOLETE	(1) obese	(2) abstruse	(3) antiquated	(4) callow
21.	SUBSTANTIATE	(1) patronize	(2) substantive	(3) confirm	(4) subsidize
22.	ASSESSMENT	(1) fund	(2) subsidy	(3) toll	(4) assignment
23.	REMUNERATION	(1) enumeration	(2) payment	(3) praise	(4) advancement

2 (#8)

#	Word	(1)	(2)	(3)	(4)
24.	TENTATIVE	conclusive	provisional	limited	simple
25.	EXPENDITURE	outlay	choice	future	purchase
26.	CHARLATAN	accessory	bystander	clerk	quack
27.	CAPITULATE	surrender	revive	adjust	assimilate
28.	DISSEMINATE	use	withdraw	spread	orate
29.	ANALOGOUS	puzzling	similar	general	false
30.	GRATUITOUSLY	freely	slowly	unwilling	quickly
31.	LENIENT	smooth	mild	rigorous	heavy
32.	RECIPROCAL	agreeable	excessive	pompous	mutual
33.	STABILITY	inconstancy	drudgery	steadfastness	laxity
34.	RETRACT	repeat	affirm	withdraw	question
35.	SPURIOUS	sham	tacit	dogmatic	thin
36.	VITIATE	improve	imitate	contaminate	antagonize
37.	TENDERED	offered	withdrawn	relied	versed
38.	VERIFICATION	denial	supplication	usefulness	confirmation
39.	VELOCITY	rate	distance	variance	identity
40.	WARRANT	plan	law	authorization	provision

PART VIII

1. 1	11. 4	21. 3	31. 2
2. 3	12. 2	22. 3	32. 4
3. 3	13. 4	23. 2	33. 3
4. 2	14. 2	24. 2	34. 3
5. 2	15. 4	25. 1	35. 1
6. 4	16. 4	26. 4	36. 3
7. 4	17. 1	27. 1	37. 1
8. 1	18. 2	28. 3	38. 4
9. 1	19. 1	29. 2	39. 1
10. 1	20. 3	30. 1	40. 3

PART IX

DIRECTIONS: Some of the following sentences contain grammatical errors. Each incorrect sentence contains only ONE error. When a sentence is incorrect, cross out the one wrong word and write the correct word at the end of the line. When a sentence is correct, be sure to write "correct" at the end of the line.

Samples:
    Do not read aloud   correct
    Where was you today?   were

1. He won't leave me come in.   1.____
2. My brother is taller than me.   2.____
3. She don't want to go home.   3.____
4. Both parts of the drawbridge raise at once.   4.____
5. Don't get this kind of gloves.   5.____
6. I have drank all my milk now.   6.____
7. Will you bring this to the office across the street?   7.____
8. Neither the president nor the manager are taking a vacation.   8.____
9. Each of them took their own books to school.   9.____
10. No one would tell who he had named.   10.____
11. This record is different from any I have every read.   11.____
12. Three of us salesmen have tied for first place.   12.____
13. The little girl's hand was hurt.   13.____
14. I wish that today was Sunday.   14.____
15. Whom did you say called to see him?   15.____
16. He was deeply affected by the loss of his brother.   16.____
17. I can't hardly realize that the bill has been passed.   17.____
18. Just between you and I, he is not to be trusted.   18.____
19. I now come to the second of the two topics.   19.____
20. Business conditions will look differently to you after you return from your vacation.   20.____
21. He is one of the best of the buyers who has been employed.   21.____
22. They proved that the work was all right.   22.____

23. Neither the boy or the girl looks like you.   23. _____

24. This phenomena is rare.   24. _____

PART IX

1. let
2. I
3. doesn't
4. rise
5. glove

6. drunk
7. correct
8. is
9. his
10. whom

11. ever
12. correct
13. correct
14. were
15. Who

16. correct
17. can
18. me
19. correct
20. different

21. correct
22. correct
23. nor
24. phenomenon

EXAMINATION SECTION
TEST 1

DIRECTIONS: Each question or incomplete statement is followed by several suggested answers or completions. Select the one that BEST answers the question or completes the statement. *PRINT THE LETTER OF THE CORRECT ANSWER IN THE SPACE AT THE RIGHT.*

Questions 1-3
For questions 1 through 3, there is a name or code provided along with four other names or codes listed in alphabetical/numerical order. Find the correct space for the given name or code so that it will be in proper order with the rest of the list.

1. Roggen, Sam   1.____

    A. _
    Rogers, Arthur L
    B. _
    Roghani, Fada
    C. _
    Rogovin, H.T.
    D. _
    Rogowski, Marie R.
    E. _

2. 05076012   2.____

    A. _
    05076004
    B. _
    05076007
    C. _
    05076010
    D. _
    05076021
    E. _

3. CBA-1875   3.____

    A. _
    CAA-1720
    B. _
    CAB-1819
    C. _
    CAC-1804
    D. _
    CAD-1402
    E. _

Questions 4-8
Questions 4 through 8 require you to compare names, addresses or codes. In each line below there are three items that are very much alike. Compare the three and answer as follows:

Answer "A" if all three are exactly alike;
Answer "B" if only the FIRST and SECOND items are exactly alike;
Answer "C" if only the FIRST and THIRD items are exactly alike;
Answer "D" if only the SECOND AND THIRD items are exactly alike;
Answer "E" if all three names are different.

4.	Helene Bedell	Helene Beddell	Helene Beddell	4.___
5.	FT. Wedemeyer	FT. Wedemeyer	FT. Wedmeyer	5.___
6.	3214 W. Beaumont St.	3214 W. Beaumount St.	3214 Beaumont St.	6.___
7.	BC3105T-5	BC3015T-5	BC3105T-5	7.___
8.	4460327	4460327	4460327	8.___

For questions 9 through 11, find the correct spelling of the word and write the correct letter in the space at the right.

9. A. accomodate   B. acommodate   9.___
    C. accommadate   D. none of the above

10. A. manageble   B. manageable   10.___
    C. manegeable   D. none of the above

11. A. reccommend   B. recommend   11.___
    C. recammend   D. none of the above

12. 32 + 26 =   12.___

    A. 69
    B. 59
    C. 58
    D. 54
    E. none of the above

13. 57-15 =   13.___

    A. 72
    B. 62
    C. 54
    D. 44
    E. none of the above

14. 23x7 =   14.___

    A. 164
    B. 161
    C. 154
    D. 141
    E. none of the above

15. 160/5 =   15.___

    A. 32

B. 30
C. 25
D. 21
E. none of the above

16. 17.8 + 13.3 =   16._____

A. 30.1
B. 31.0
C. 31.1
D. 33.3

Questions 17-19

Questions 17 through 19 test the ability to follow instructions. Following the directions in each item will lead you to identify or create a specific letter-number combination. Next, use the "Look-Up Table" to find the letter that corresponds with your letter-number combination. Mark this letter in the space at the right.

For example, if the combination is "P1," the answer would be "A" because this is the letter indicated in the box where "P" and "1" meet in the table.

LOOK-UP TABLE					
	P	Q	R	S	T
1	A	B	c,	D	E
2	B	C	D	E	A
3	C	D	E	A	B
4	D	E	A	B	C
5	E	A	B	C	D
6-	A	B	C	D	E
7	B	C	D	E	A
8	C	D	E	A	B
9	D	E	A	B	C
10	E	A	B	C	D

17. Look at the letter-number combinations below. Draw a circle around the third combina-   17._____
tion from the left. Write that letter-number combination in this space: _____
   T1   S5   P2   Q5   P5   R2

18. Draw a line under each letter that appears only once in the line. Write the letter "Q" and   18._____
the number of lines you drew here: _____
   S T Q T Q P T Q

19. Look again at the line of letters in question 16. Draw a circle around each "Q." Write the   19._____
letter that appears at the beginning of the line and the number of circles you drew here:

_____

20. Select the sentence which is MOST APPROPRIATE with respect to grammar, usage and   20._____
punctuation suitable for a formal letter or report:

A. Major repairs has caused the cafeteria to be closed until late October.
B. The cafeteria will be closed until late October on account of major repairs.

C. The cafeteria will be closed for major repairs until late October.
D. The closing of the cafeteria until late October due to the completion of major repairs.

In questions 21 through 23, identify the most similar meaning to the highlighted word:

21. The staff was **amazed** by the news.

    A. pleased
    B. surprised
    C. saddened
    D. relieved

22. Please **delete** the second paragraph.

    A. retype
    B. reread
    C. revise
    D. remove

23. Did you **duplicate** the information as written?

    A. type
    B. copy
    C. remember
    D. understand

24. "It is a simple matter to find and correct the errors made by a typist, but often a file clerk's errors are not discovered until something which is needed cannot be found. For this reason, the work of every file clerk should be checked at regular intervals."
    The paragraph BEST supports the statement that filing

    A. may contain errors that are not immediately noticeable
    B. should be organized by typists rather than file clerks
    C. is a more difficult process than typing
    D. should be checked for errors more frequently than typing

25. "The most efficient method for performing a task is not always easily determined. That which is economical in terms of time must be carefully distinguished from that which is economical in terms of expended energy. In short, the quickest method may require a degree of physical effort that may be neither essential nor desirable." The paragraph BEST supports the statement that

    A. it is more efficient to perform a task slowly than rapidly
    B. skill in performing a task should not be acquired at the expense of time
    C. the most efficient execution of a task is not always the one done in the shortest time
    D. energy and time cannot both be considered in the performance of a single task

KEY (CORRECT ANSWERS)

1.	B	11.	B
2.	D	12.	C
3.	E	13.	E
4.	D	14.	B
5.	B	15.	A
6.	E	16.	C
7.	C	17.	B
8.	A	18.	C
9.	D	19.	A
10.	B	20.	C

21. B
22. D
23. B
24. A
25. C

EXAMINATION SECTION
TEST 1

Memory for Addresses Test

DIRECTIONS: In this test you will have to memorize the locations (A, B, C, D or E) of 25 addresses shown in five boxes. For example, "Sardis" is in box "C," "4300-4799 West" is in box "E," etc. Study the locations of the addresses for five minutes (try sounding them to yourself), then cover the boxes and try to answer the questions below. *PRINT THE LETTER OF THE CORRECT ANSWER IN THE SPACE AT THE RIGHT.*

Box A	Box B	Box C
4700-5599 Table	6800-6999 Table	5600-6499 Table
Lismore	Kelford	Joel
4800-5199 West	5200-5799 West	3200-3499 West
Hesper	Musella	Sardis
5500-6399 Blake	4800-5499 Blake	6400-7299 Blake

Box D	Box E
6500-6799 Table	4400-4699 Table
Tatum	Ruskin
3500-4299 West	4300-4799 West
Porter	Somers
4300-4799 Blake	7300-7499 Blake

1. Musella   1._____
2. 4300-4799 Blake   2._____
3. 4700-5599 Table   3._____
4. Tatum   4._____
5. 5500-6399 Blake   5._____
6. Hesper   6._____
7. Kelford   7._____
8. Somers   8._____
9. 6400-7299 Blake   9._____
10. Joel   10._____
11. 5500-6399 Blake   11._____
12. 5200-5799 West   12._____
13. Porter   13._____
14. 7300-7499 Blake   14._____

KEY (CORRECT ANSWERS)

1. B
2. D
3. A
4. D
5. A
6. A
7. B
8. E
9. C
10. C
11. A
12. B
13. D
14. E

TEST 2

Address Checking Test

DIRECTIONS: In this test you will have to decide whether two addresses are alike or different. If the two addresses are exactly alike in every way, mark the answer "A." If the two addresses are different, mark the answer "D." *PRINT THE LETTER OF THE CORRECT ANSWER IN THE SPACE AT THE RIGHT.*

1. 2134 S. 20th St.   2134 S. 20th St.   1.____
2. 4608 N. Warnock St.   4806 N. Warnock St.   2.____
3. 1202 W. Girard Dr.   1202 W. Girard Rd.   3.____
4. Chappaqua, NY 10514   Chappaqua, NY 10514   4.____
5. 2207 Markland Ave.   2207 Markham Ave.   5.____

General Test

DIRECTIONS: In this test there are three kinds of questions—Vocabulary, Reading and Number Series. For Vocabulary questions, like number 6, choose the suggested answer that means most nearly the same as the word or words in italics. For Reading questions, like number 7, read the paragraph and answer the question that follows it. For Number Series questions, like numbers 8 through 25, there is a series of numbers which is arranged in some definite order or pattern, followed by five sets of two numbers each. Determine the order or pattern of the numbers at the left and choose from the selections below the two numbers that would properly continue the order or pattern. *PRINT THE LETTER OF THE CORRECT ANSWER IN THE SPACE AT THE RIGHT.*

6. The reports were *consolidated by* the secretary. *Consolidated* most nearly means   6.____

    A. combined   B. concluded   C. distributed   D. protected   E. weighed

7. "Post office clerks assigned to stamp windows are directly responsible financially in the selling of postage. In addition, they are expected to have a thorough knowledge as to the acceptability of matter offered for mailing. Any information which they give out to the public must be accurate."   7.____
The paragraph best supports the statement that clerks assigned to stamp-window duty

    A. must account for stamps issued to them for sale
    B. have had long training in other post-office work
    C. advise the public only on matters of official business
    D. must refer continuously to the sources of postal regulations
    E. inspect the contents of every package offered for mailing

8. 1 2 3 4 5 6 7 ...   8.____
    A. 1 2   B. 5 6   C. 8 9
    D. 4 5   E. 7 8

2 (#2)

9. 15 14 13 12 11 10 9 ...

    A. 2 1   B. 17 16   C. 8 9
    D. 8 7   E. 9 8

9. _____

10. 20 20 21 21 22 22 23 ...

    A. 23 23   B. 23 24   C. 19 19
    D. 22 23   E. 21 22

10. _____

11. 17 3 17 4 17 5 17 ...

    A. 6 17   B. 6 7   C. 17 6
    D. 5 6   E. 17 7

11. _____

12. 1 2 4 5 7 8 10 ...

    A. 11 12   B. 12 14   C. 10 13
    D. 12 13   E. 11 13

12. _____

13. 21 21 20 20 19 19 18 ...

    A. 18 18   B. 18 17   C. 17 18
    D. 17 17   E. 18 19

13. _____

14. 1 22 1 23 1 24 1 ...

    A. 26 1   B. 25 26   C. 25 1
    D. 1 26   E. 1 25

14. _____

15. 1 20 3 19 5 18 7 ...

    A. 8 9   B. 8 17   C. 17 10
    D. 17 9   E. 9 18

15. _____

16. 4 7 10 13 16 19 22 ...

    A. 23 26   B. 25 27   C. 25 26
    D. 25 28   E. 24 27

16. _____

17. 30 2 28 4 26 6 24 ...

    A. 23 9   B. 26 8   C. 8 9
    D. 26 22   E. 8 22

17. _____

18. 5 6 20 7 8 19 9 ...

    A. 10 18   B. 18 17   C. 10 7
    D. 18 19   E. 10 11

18. _____

19. 9 10 1 11 12 2 13 ...

    A. 2 14   B. 3 14   C. 14 3
    D. 14 15   E. 14 1

19. _____

20. 4 6 9 11 14 16 19 ...

    A. 21 24   B. 22 25   C. 20 22
    D. 21 23   E. 22 24

20. _____

21. 8 8 1 10 10 3 12 ...   21._____

    A. 13 13   B. 12 5   C. 12 4
    D. 13 5   E. 4 12

22. 14 1 2 15 3 4 16...   22._____

    A. 5 16   B. 6 7   C. 5 17
    D. 5 6   E. 17 5

23. 10 12 50 15 17 50 20 ...   23._____

    A. 50 21   B. 21 50   C. 50 22
    D. 22 50   E. 22 24

24. 1 2 3 50 4 5 6 51 7 8...   24._____

    A. 9 10   B. 9 52   C. 51 10
    D. 10 52   E. 10 50

25. 20 21 23 24 27 28 32 33 38 39 ...   25._____

    A. 45 46   B. 45 52   C. 44 45
    D. 44 49   E. 40 46

KEY (CORRECT ANSWERS)

1.	A	11.	A
2.	D	12.	E
3.	D	13.	B
4.	A	14.	C
5.	D	15.	D
6.	A	16.	D
7.	A	17.	E
8.	C	18.	A
9.	D	19.	C
10.	B	20.	A

21. B
22. D
23. D
24. B
25. A

NAME AND NUMBER COMPARISONS

COMMENTARY

This test seeks to measure your ability and disposition to do a job carefully and accurately, your attention to exactness and preciseness of detail, your alertness and versatility in discerning similarities and differences between things, and your power in systematically handling written language symbols.

It is actually a test of your ability to do academic and/or clerical work, using the basic elements of verbal (qualitative) and mathematical (quantitative) learning—words and numbers.

EXAMINATION SECTION

TEST 1

DIRECTIONS: In each line across the page there are three names or numbers that are much alike. Compare the three names or numbers and decide which ones are exactly alike. *PRINT IN THE SPACE AT THE RIGHT THE LETTER:*
  A. if all THREE names or numbers are exactly alike
  B. if only the FIRST and SECOND names or numbers are ALIKE
  C. if only the FIRST and THIRD names or numbers are alike
  D. if only the SECOND or THIRD names or numbers are alike
  E. if ALL THREE names or numbers are DIFFERENT

1.	Davis Hazen	David Hozen	David Hazen	1.____
2.	Lois Appel	Lois Appel	Lois Apfel	2.____
3.	June Allan	Jane Allan	Jane Allan	3.____
4.	10235	10235	10235	4.____
5.	32614	32164	32614	5.____

TEST 2

1.	2395890	2395890	2395890	1.____
2.	1926341	1926347	1926314	2.____
3.	E. Owens McVey	E. Owen McVey	E. Owen McVay	3.____
4.	Emily Neal Rouse	Emily Neal Rowse	Emily Neal Rowse	4.____
5.	H. Merritt Audubon	H. Merriott Audubon	H. Merritt Audubon	5.____

TEST 3

1. 6219354	6219354	6219354	1.____
2. 231793	2312793	2312793	2.____
3. 1065407	1065407	1065047	3.____
4. Francis Ransdell	Frances Ramsdell	Francis Ramsdell	4.____
5. Cornelius Detwiler	Cornelius Detwiler	Cornelius Detwiler	5.____

TEST 4

1. 6452054	6452564	6542054	1.____
2. 8501268	8501268	8501286	2.____
3. Ella Burk Newham	Ella Burk Newnham	Elena Burk Newnham	3.____
4. Jno. K. Ravencroft	Jno. H. Ravencroft	Jno. H. Ravencoft	4.____
5. Martin Wills Pullen	Martin Wills Pulen	Martin Wills Pullen	5.____

TEST 5

1. 3457988	3457986	3457986	1.____
2. 4695682	4695862	4695682	2.____
3. Stricklund Kaneydy	Sticklund Kanedy	Stricklund Kanedy	3.____
4. Joy Harlor Witner	Joy Harloe Witner	Joy Harloe Witner	4.____
5. R.M.O. Uberroth	R.M.O. Uberroth	R.N.O. Uberroth	5.____

TEST 6

1. 1592514	1592574	1592574	1.____
2. 2010202	2010202	2010220	2.____
3. 6177396	6177936	6177396	3.____
4. Drusilla S. Ridgeley	Drusilla S. Ridgeley	Drusilla S. Ridgeley	4.____
5. Andrei I. Tooumantzev	Andrei I. Tourmantzev	Andrei I. Toumantzov	5.____

TEST 7

1. 5261383	5261383	5261338	1.____
2. 8125690	8126690	8125609	2.____
3. W.E. Johnston	W.E. Johnson	W.E. Johnson	3.____
4. Vergil L. Muller	Vergil L. Muller	Vergil L. Muller	4.____
5. Atherton R. Warde	Asheton R. Warde	Atherton P. Warde	5.____

TEST 8

1. 013469.5	023469.5	02346.95	1.____
2. 33376	333766	333766	2.____
3. Ling-Temco-Vought	Ling-Tenco-Vought	Ling-Temco Vought	3.____
4. Lorilard Corp.	Lorillard Corp.	Lorrilard Corp.	4.____
5. American Agronomics Corporation	American Agronomics Corporation	American Agronomic Corporation	5.____

TEST 9

1.	436592864	436592864	436592864	1.____
2.	197765123	197755123	197755123	2.____
3.	Dewaay Cortvriendt International S.A.	Deway Cortvriendt International S.A.	Deway Corturiendt International S.A.	3.____
4.	Crédit Lyonnais	Crèdit Lyonnais	Crèdit Lyonais	4.____
5.	Algemene Bank Nederland N.V.	Algamene Bank Nederland N.V.	Algemene Bank Naderland N.V.	5.____

TEST 10

1.	00032572	0.0032572	00032522	1.____
2.	399745	399745	398745	2.____
3.	Banca Privata Finanziaria S.p.A.	Banca Privata Finanzaria S.P.A.	Banca Privata Finanziaria S.P.A.	3.____
4.	Eastman Dillon, Union Securities & Co.	Eastman Dillon, Union Securities Co.	Eastman Dillon, Union Securities & Co.	4.____
5.	Arnhold and S. Bleichroeder, Inc.	Arnhold & S. Bleichroeder, Inc.	Arnold and S. Bleichroeder, Inc.	5.____

TEST 11

DIRECTIONS: Answer the questions below on the basis of the following instructions: For each such numbered set of names, addresses, and numbers listed in Columns I and II, select your answer from the following options:
- A. The names in Columns I and II are different
- B. The addresses in Columns I and II are different
- C. The numbers in Columns I and II are different
- D. The names, addresses and numbers are identical

1. Francis Jones
   62 Stately Avenue
   96-12446

   Francis Jones
   62 Stately Avenue
   96-21446

   1._____

2. Julio Montez
   19 Ponderosa Road
   56-73161

   Julio Montez
   19 Ponderosa Road
   56-71361

   2._____

3. Mary Mitchell
   2314 Melbourne Drive
   68-92172

   Mary Mitchell
   2314 Melbourne Drive
   68-92172

   3._____

4. Harry Patterson
   25 Dunne Street
   14-33430

   Harry Patterson
   25 Dunne Street
   14-34330

   4._____

5. Patrick Murphy
   171 West Hosmer Street
   93-81214

   Patrick Murphy
   171 West Hosmer Street
   93-18214

   5._____

TEST 12

1. August Schultz
816 St. Clair Avenue
53-40149

   August Schultz
816 St. Claire Avenue
53-40149

   1.____

2. George Taft
72 Runnymede Street
47-04033

   George Taft
72 Runnymede Street
47-04023

   2.____

3. Angus Henderson
1418 Madison Street
81-76375

   Angus Henderson
1418 Madison Street
81-76375

   3.____

4. Carolyn Mazur
12 Rivenlew Road
38-99615

   Carolyn Mazur
12 Rivervane Road
38-99615

   4.____

5. Adele Russell
1725 Lansing Lane
72-91962

   Adela Russell
1725 Lansing Lane
72-91962

   5.____

TEST 13

DIRECTIONS: The following questions are based on the instructions given below. In each of the following questions, the 3-line name and address in Column I is the master-list entry, and the 3-line entry in Column II is the information to be checked against the master list.
If there is one line that is NOT exactly alike, mark your answer A.
If there are two lines NOT exactly alike, mark your answer B.
If there are three lines NOT exactly alike, mark your answer C.
If the lines ALL are exactly alike, mark your answer D.

1. Jerome A. Jackson
    1243 14th Avenue
    New York, N.Y. 10023

    Jerome A. Johnson
    1234 14th Avenue
    New York, N.Y. 10023

    1.____

2. Sophie Strachtheim
    33-28 Connecticut Ave.
    Far Rockaway, N.Y. 11697

    Sophie Strachtheim
    33-28 Connecticut Ave.
    Far Rockaway, N.Y. 11697

    2.____

3. Elisabeth NT. Gorrell
    256 Exchange St
    New York, N.Y. 10013

    Elizabeth NT. Correll
    256 Exchange St.
    New York, N.Y. 10013

    3.____

4. Maria J. Gonzalez
    7516 E. Sheepshead Rd.
    Brooklyn, N.Y. 11240

    Maria J. Gonzalez
    7516 N. Shepshead Rd.
    Brooklyn, N.Y. 11240

    4.____

5. Leslie B. Brautenweiler
    21-57A Seller Terr.
    Flushing, N.Y. 11367

    Leslie B. Brautenwieler
    21-75ASeiler Terr.
    Flushing, N.J. 11367

    5.____

KEY (CORRECT ANSWERS)

TEST 1	TEST 2	TEST 3	TEST 4	TEST 5	TEST 6	TEST 7
1. E	1. A	1. A	1. E	1. D	1. D	1. B
2. B	2. E	2. A	2. B	2. C	2. B	2. E
3. D	3. E	3. B	3. E	3. E	3. C	3. D
4. A	4. D	4. E	4. E	4. D	4. A	4. A
5. C	5. C	5. A	5. C	5. B	5. E	5. E

TEST 8	TEST 9	TEST 10	TEST 11	TEST 12	TEST 13
1. E	1. A	1. E	1. C	1. B	1. B
2. D	2. D	2. B	2. C	2. C	2. D
3. E	3. E	3. E	3. D	3. D	3. A
4. E	4. E	4. C	4. C	4. B	4. A
5. B	5. E	5. E	5. C	5. A	5. C

EXAMINATION SECTION
TEST 1

DIRECTIONS: Each question or incomplete statement is followed by several suggested answers or completions. Select the one that BEST answers the question or completes the statement. *PRINT THE LETTER OF THE CORRECT ANSWER IN THE SPACE AT THE RIGHT.*

Questions 1-25.

DIRECTIONS: Questions 1 through 25 refer to the rate charts at the end of this test. Use the appropriate chart to answer these questions.

1. What is the cost of one letter weighing 4 ounces and two letters weighing 8 ounces apiece when all three letters are mailed at the carrier route first-class rate?   1.____
   A. $63.75   B. $63.81   C. $63.87   D. $63.93   E. $63.99

2. Three single postcards and four double postcards cost   2.____
   A. $1.65   B. $1.70   C. $1.75   D. $1.80   E. $1.85

3. One first-class parcel weighing 36 pounds being sent to Zone 4 and one first-class 15-pound parcel being sent to Zone 6 cost   3.____
   A. $32.48   B. $32.70   C. $35.78   D. $36.14   E. $36.64

4. What is the cost of two books at the special fourth-class rates using the single piece rate with one book weighing 4.5 pounds and the other book weighing 1 pound?   4.____
   A. $2.15   B. $2.50   C. $2.85   D. $3.20   E. $3.55

5. Three first-class letters weighing 3 ounces, 5 ounces, and 7 ounces, respectively, cost   5.____
   A. $2.75   B. $2.85   C. $2.95   D. $3.05   E. $3.15

6. Four first-class letters weighing 5.2 ounces apiece and five single postcards cost   6.____
   A. $5.20   B. $5.75   C. $4.40   D. $4.95   E. $4.80

7. Three books at library rates which weigh 11 ounces, 4 pounds, and 7 pounds 3 ounces, respectively, cost   7.____
   A. $3.95   B. $4.11   C. $5.04   D. $5.97   E. $6.90

8. Six first-class letters at the zip+4 nonpresort rates-two letters weighing 2 ounces apiece, and the other four letters weighing 3 ounces apiece cost   8.____
   A. $4.65   B. $3.85   C. $4.25   D. $3.05   E. $3.45

9. Three first-class letters weighing 9 ounces apiece and five first-class letters weighing 8.4 ounces apiece cost   9.____
   A. $13.20   B. $13.80   C. $14.80   D. $16.20   E. $17.70

2 (#1)

10. One 25-pound first-class parcel, one 40-pound first-class parcel, and two 10-pound first-class parcels, all being sent locally, cost   10.____

    A. $42.48   B. $43.52   C. $44.76   D. $45.18   E. $46.50

11. Two letters weighing 10 ounces apiece and one single postcard, all of which are being mailed at the carrier route first-class rate, cost   11.____

    A. $63.51   B. $63.71   C. $63.91   D. $64.11   E. $64.31

12. Four books are sent at the special fourth-class rates. One book weighs 8 pounds and is being mailed at the single piece rate. The other three books weigh 3 pounds apiece and are being mailed at the Level A presort rate. The total cost is   12.____

    A. $7.25   B. $7.75   C. $8.25   D. $8.75   E. $9.25

13. One 18-pound parcel being sent to Zone 5, one 50-pound parcel being sent to Zone 3, and three 4-pound parcels being sent to Zone 6 cost   13.____

    A. $49.66   B. $50.12   C. $50.30   D. $51.48   E. $51.94

14. Two 5-ounce letters and one single postcard, all being mailed first class at the presort rate, cost   14.____

    A. $62.07   B. $61.94   C. $61.81   D. $61.68   E. $61.55

15. Eight books are sent at library rates. Three books weigh 2 pounds apiece, three books weigh 6 pounds apiece, and the last two books weigh 9 pounds apiece.
The total cost is   15.____

    A. $9.89   B. $10.76   C. $11.63   D. $12.50   E. $13.37

16. Ten first-class letters are sent at the zip+4 presort rates. Five letters weigh 4 ounces apiece, four letters weigh 7 ounces apiece, and the last letter weighs 2 ounces. What is the total cost?   16.____

    A. $74.07   B. $74.27   C. $74.47   D. $74.67   E. $74.87

17. Three 16-pound parcels being sent to Zone 8 and four 20-pound parcels being sent to Zone 4 cost   17.____

    A. $95.97   B. $96.25   C. $99.13   D. $102.71   E. $105.93

18. Four letters weighing 1.8 ounces apiece and two letters weighing 12 ounces apiece, all being mailed at the carrier route first-class rate, cost   18.____

    A. $65.97   B. $66.05   C. $66.13   D. $66.21   E. $66.29

19. Seven letters weighing 8 ounces apiece being mailed first class at the presort rate cost   19.____

    A. $69.59   B. $70.29   C. $70.99   D. $71.69   E. $72.39

20. Nine first-class letters are sent at the zip+4 rates. Three of these weigh 9 ounces apiece and are being mailed at the presort rates; the other six letters weigh 4 ounces apiece and are being mailed at the nonpresort rates.
The total cost is   20.____

    A. $69.87   B. $70.17   C. $70.47   D. $70.77   E. $71.07

3 (#1)

21. One 30-pound parcel is mailed to Zone 6, and three 4-pound books are mailed fourth class at the single piece rate.
    The total cost is

    A. $30.40   B. $30.95   C. $31.50   D. $32.05   E. $32.60

22. Ten books are being mailed fourth class at the Level B rates, and five books are being mailed at the library rates. Each of the books weighs 8 pounds apiece.
    The total cost is

    A. $33.30   B. $36.20   C. $39.10   D. $42.00   E. $44.90

23. Four 45-pound parcels are being mailed to Zone 2, and two 14-pound books are being mailed at the library rates.
    The total cost is

    A. $88.36   B. $88.48   C. $88.60   D. $88.72   E. $88.84

24. Two first-class letters weighing 3 ounces apiece and five presorted first-class letters weighing 2 ounces apiece are brought to your counter.
    The total cost is

    A. $62.95   B. $63.15   C. $63.35   D. $63.55   E. $63.75

25. Three 10-pound parcels are being mailed to Zone 4, two books are being mailed fourth class at the Level A rates, and six books are being mailed at the library rates. Each book weighs 5 pounds.
    The total cost is

    A. $34.95   B. $35.17   C. $35.40   D. $35.63   E. $35.86

KEY (CORRECT ANSWERS)

1. C
2. A
3. C
4. D
5. E

6. B
7. B
8. E
9. C
10. A

11. D
12. A
13. C
14. A
15. D

16. B
17. E
18. E
19. C
20. C

21. B
22. D
23. B
24. C
25. D

SOLUTIONS TO PROBLEMS

1. Using Chart G, $60.00 + 0.755 + (2)(1.555) - $63.87 (Ans. C)
2. Using Chart B, (3)(0.15) + (4)(0.30) = $1.65 (Ans. A)
3. Using Chart J, 22.42 + 13.36 = $35.78 (Ans. C)
4. Using Exhibit 711.32, 2.30 + 0.90 = $3.20 (Ans. D)
5. Using Chart A, 0.65 + 1.05 + 1.45 = $3.15 (Ans. E)
6. Using Charts A, B, (4)(1.25) + (5)(0.15) = $5.75 (Ans. B)
7. Using Exhibit 711.42, 0.64 + 1.33 + 2.14 = $4.11 (Ans. B)
8. Using Chart C, (2)(0.441) + (4)(0.641) = 3.446 or $3.45 (Ans. E)
9. Using Chart A, (3)(1.85) + (5)(1.85) = $14.80 (Ans. C)
10. Using Chart J, 12.21 + 18.57 + (2)(5.85) = $42.48 (Ans. A)
11. Using Chart G, 60.00 + (2)(1.995) + 0.115 = $64.11 (Ans. D)
12. Using Exhibit 711.32, 3.20 + (3)(1.35) = $7.25 (Ans. A)
13. Using Chart J, 13.90 + 22.81 + (3)(4.53) = $50.30 (Ans. C)
14. Using Chart D, 60.00 + (2)(0.97) + 0.13 = $62.07 (Ans. A)
15. Using Exhibit 711.42, (3)(0.87) + (3)(1.79) + (2)(2.26) = $12.50 (Ans. D)
16. Using Chart E, 60.00 + (5)(0.805) + (4)(1.405) + 0.405 = $74.27 (Ans. B)
17. Using Chart J, (3)(17.75) + (4)(13.17) - $105.93 (Ans. E)
18. Using Chart G, 60.00 + (4)(0.395) + (2)(2.355) = $66.29 (Ans. E)
19. Using Chart D, 60.00 + (7)(1.57) = $70.99 (Ans. C)
20. UsingCharts E,C,60.00 + (3)(1.805) + (6)(0.841) = 70.461 or $70.47 (Ans. C)
21. Using Chart J, Exh. 711.32, 25.10 + (3)(1.95) - $30.95 (Ans. B)
22. Using Exhibits 711.32, 711.42, (10)(3.13) + (5)(2.14) = $42.00 (Ans. D)
23. Using Chart J, Exh. 711.42, (4)(20.69) + (2)(2.86) = $88.48 (Ans. B)
24. Using Charts A, D, (2)(0.65) + 60.00 + (5)(0.41) = $63.35 (Ans. C)
25. Using Chart J, Exh. 711.32, Exh. 711.42, (3)(7.39) + (2)(2.05) + (6)(1.56) = $35.63 (Ans. D)

Exhibit 310 (p. 1)

First-Class Mail

310 Rates and Fees
(See Exhibit 310)

A. Single Pieces 11 ounces or less (Other Than Postal Cards or Postcards):
This applies to First-Class pieces other than postal or post cards that do not exceed 11 ounces:
- First ounce or fraction of an ounce $0.25
- Each additional ounce or fraction of an ounce . . 0.20

Weight Not Exceeding (Ounces)	Rate
1	$0.25
2	0.45
3	0.65
4	0.85
5	1.05
6	1.25
7	1.45
8	1.65
9	1.85
10	2.05
11	2.25

B. Cards:
Postal cards are stamped cards sold by the USPS. Postcards are sold commercially and need to have stamps added. Rates:
Postal cards:
- Single . . . . $.15 each
- Double . . . . $.30 ($.15 each part)

Postcards:
- Single . . . . $.15 each
- Double . . . . $.30 ($.15 each part)

(Reply part does not have to bear postage when originally mailed.)

C. Nonpresorted ZIP + 4 First-Class Mail:
Rates for matter other than cards: $0.241 for the first ounce, and $0.20 for each additional ounce or fraction.
Rates for Cards: $0.141 each.

D. Presorted First-Class Mail:
To mail at Presorted First-Class rates, the annual presort fee of $60 must first be paid. (Payment of one $60 fee allows the mailer to mail qualifying matter at all First-Class presort rates including Carrier Route First-Class, ZIP + 4 Presort, and ZIP + 4 Barcoded.)
Rates Per Piece for Matter Other than Cards:
Pieces weighing two ounces or less: $0.21 for the first ounce or fraction and $0.20 for the second ounce or fraction.
Pieces weighing over two ounces: $0.17 for the first ounce or fraction and $0.20 for each additional ounce or fraction.
Rates Per Piece for Cards: $0.13

E. ZIP + 4 Presort First-Class Mail
To mail at the ZIP + 4 Presort rate, the annual presort fee of $60 must be paid. (Payment of one $60 fee allows the mailer to mail qualifying matter at all First-Class presort rates including Presorted First-Class, Carrier Route First-Class, and ZIP + 4 Barcoded.)
Rates Per Piece for Matter Other than Cards:
First Ounce or Fraction: $0.205
Each Additional Ounce or Fraction: $0.20
Rate Per Piece for Cards: $0.125

F. ZIP + 4 Barcoded First-Class Mail:
To mail at the ZIP + 4 Barcoded rate, the annual presort fee of $60 must be paid. (Payment of one $60 fee allows the mailer to mail qualifying matter at all First-Class presort rates including Presorted First-Class, Carrier Route First-Class, and ZIP + 4 Presort.)
Rates Per Piece for Matter Other than Cards:
First Ounce or Fraction: $0.20
Each Additional Ounce or Fraction: $0.20
Rate Per Piece for Cards: $0.12

G. Carrier Route First-Class Mail
To mail at the Carrier Route First-Class rate, the annual presort fee of $60 must first be paid. (Payment of one $60 fee allows the mailer to mail qualifying matter at all First-Class presort rates including Presorted First-Class, ZIP + 4 Presort, and ZIP + 4 Barcoded.)
Rates Per Piece for Matter Other than Cards:
Pieces weighing two ounces or less: $0.195 for the first ounce or fraction and $0.20 for the second ounce or fraction.
Pieces weighing over two ounces: $0.155 for the first ounce or fraction and $0.20 for each additional ounce or fraction.
Rate for Cards: $0.115

H. Nonstandard Surcharge
This applies to all First-Class Mail pieces weighing 1 ounce or less that exceed the size limits in 353.3, except for pieces mailed at the nonpresorted ZIP + 4, ZIP + 4 Presort, and ZIP + 4 Barcoded rates.
Rates: A surcharge of $0.10 is assessed on each piece of nonstandard First-Class Mail which is mailed at the single-piece rates for cards or for matter other than cards. A surcharge of $0.05 is assessed on each piece of nonstandard mail which is mailed at the Presorted First-Class or Carrier Route First-Class Rates.

I. Address Correction Service Fee:
The fee for address correction service is $0.30 per notice issued.

Exhibit 310 (p. 1)—First-Class Rates and Fees

Exhibit 310 (p.2)

Weight, not exceeding pound(s)	J. Priority Mail Zone/Rate					
	1, 2, & 3	4	5	6	7	8
1	2.40	2.40	2.40	2.40	2.40	2.40
2	2.40	2.40	2.40	2.40	2.40	2.40
3	2.74	3.16	3.45	3.74	3.96	4.32
4	3.18	3.75	4.13	4.53	4.92	5.33
5	3.61	4.32	4.86	5.27	5.81	6.37
6	4.15	5.08	5.71	6.31	6.91	7.66
7	4.58	5.66	6.39	7.09	7.80	8.67
8	5.00	6.23	7.07	7.87	8.68	9.68
9	5.43	6.81	7.76	8.66	9.57	10.69
10	5.85	7.39	8.44	9.44	10.45	11.70
11	6.27	7.97	9.12	10.22	11.33	12.71
12	6.70	8.55	9.81	11.01	12.22	13.72
13	7.12	9.12	10.49	11.79	13.10	14.73
14	7.55	9.70	11.17	12.57	13.99	15.74
15	7.97	10.28	11.86	13.36	14.87	16.75
16	8.39	10.86	12.54	14.14	15.75	17.75
17	8.82	11.44	13.22	14.92	16.64	18.76
18	9.24	12.01	13.90	15.70	17.52	19.77
19	9.67	12.59	14.59	16.49	18.41	20.78
20	10.09	13.17	15.27	17.27	19.29	21.79
21	10.51	13.75	15.95	18.05	20.17	22.80
22	10.94	14.33	16.64	18.84	21.06	23.81
23	11.36	14.90	17.32	19.62	21.94	24.82
24	11.79	15.48	18.00	20.40	22.83	25.83
25	12.21	16.06	18.69	21.19	23.71	26.84
26	12.63	16.64	19.37	21.97	24.59	27.84
27	13.06	17.22	20.05	22.75	25.48	28.85
28	13.48	17.79	20.73	23.53	26.36	29.86
29	13.91	18.37	21.42	24.32	27.25	30.87
30	14.33	18.95	22.10	25.10	28.13	31.88
31	14.75	19.53	22.78	25.88	29.01	32.89
32	15.18	20.11	23.47	26.67	29.90	33.90
33	15.60	20.68	24.15	27.45	30.78	34.91
34	16.03	21.26	24.83	28.23	31.67	35.92
35	16.45	21.84	25.52	29.02	32.55	36.93
36	16.87	22.42	26.20	29.80	33.43	37.93
37	17.30	23.00	26.88	30.58	34.32	38.94
38	17.72	23.57	27.56	31.36	35.20	39.95
39	18.15	24.15	28.25	32.15	36.09	40.96
40	18.57	24.73	28.93	32.93	36.97	41.97
41	18.99	25.31	29.61	33.71	37.85	42.98
42	19.42	25.89	30.30	34.50	38.74	43.99
43	19.84	26.46	30.98	35.28	39.62	45.00
44	20.27	27.04	31.66	36.06	40.51	46.01
45	20.69	27.62	32.35	36.85	41.39	47.02
46	21.11	28.20	33.03	37.63	42.27	48.02
47	21.54	28.78	33.71	38.41	43.16	49.03
48	21.96	29.35	34.39	39.19	44.04	50.04
49	22.39	29.93	35.08	39.98	44.93	51.05
50	22.81	30.51	35.76	40.76	45.81	52.06
51	23.23	31.09	36.44	41.54	46.69	53.07
52	23.66	31.67	37.13	42.33	47.58	54.08
53	24.08	32.24	37.81	43.11	48.46	55.09
54	24.51	32.82	38.49	43.89	49.35	56.10
55	24.93	33.40	39.18	44.68	50.23	57.11
56	25.35	33.98	39.86	45.46	51.11	58.11
57	25.78	34.56	40.54	46.24	52.00	59.12
58	26.20	35.13	41.22	47.02	52.88	60.13
59	26.63	35.71	41.91	47.81	53.77	61.14
60	27.05	36.29	42.59	48.59	54.65	62.15
61	27.47	36.87	43.27	49.37	55.53	63.16
62	27.90	37.45	43.96	50.16	56.42	64.17
63	28.32	38.02	44.64	50.94	57.30	65.18
64	28.75	38.60	45.32	51.72	58.19	66.19
65	29.17	39.18	46.01	52.51	59.07	67.20
66	29.59	39.76	46.69	53.29	59.95	68.20
67	30.02	40.34	47.37	54.07	60.84	69.21
68	30.44	40.91	48.05	54.85	61.72	70.22
69	30.87	41.49	48.74	55.64	62.61	71.23
70	31.29	42.07	49.42	56.42	63.49	72.24

Exception: Parcels weighing less than 15 pounds, measuring over 84 inches in length and girth combined, are chargeable with a minimum rate equal to that for a 15 pound parcel for the zone to which addressed.

Exhibit 310 (p. 2), First-Class Rates and Fees

Weight Not Exceeding (Lbs.)	Single Piece Rate	Level A Presort	Level B Presort	Weight Not Exceeding (Lbs.)	Single Piece Rate	Level A Presort	Level B Presort
1	$.90	$.65	$.83	36	$8.80	$8.55	$8.73
2	1.25	1.00	1.18	37	9.00	8.75	8.93
3	1.60	1.35	1.53	38	9.20	8.95	9.13
4	1.95	1.70	1.88	39	9.40	9.15	9.33
5	2.30	2.05	2.23	40	9.60	9.35	9.53
6	2.65	2.40	2.58	41	9.80	9.55	9.73
7	3.00	2.75	2.93	42	10.00	9.75	9.93
8	3.20	2.95	3.13	43	10.20	9.95	10.13
9	3.40	3.15	3.33	44	10.40	10.15	10.33
10	3.60	3.35	3.53	45	10.60	10.35	10.53
11	3.80	3.55	3.73	46	10.80	10.55	10.73
12	4.00	3.75	3.93	47	11.00	10.75	10.93
13	4.20	3.95	4.13	48	11.20	10.95	11.13
14	4.40	4.15	4.33	49	11.40	11.15	11.33
15	4.60	4.35	4.53	50	11.60	11.35	11.53
16	4.80	4.55	4.73	51	11.80	11.55	11.73
17	5.00	4.75	4.93	52	12.00	11.75	11.93
18	5.20	4.95	5.13	53	12.20	11.95	12.13
19	5.40	5.15	5.33	54	12.40	12.15	12.33
20	5.60	5.35	5.53	55	12.60	12.35	12.53
21	5.80	5.55	5.73	56	12.80	12.55	12.73
22	6.00	5.75	5.93	57	13.00	12.75	12.93
23	6.20	5.95	6.13	58	13.20	12.95	13.13
24	6.40	6.15	6.33	59	13.40	13.15	13.33
25	6.60	6.35	6.53	60	13.60	13.35	13.53
26	6.80	6.55	6.73	61	13.80	13.55	13.73
27	7.00	6.75	6.93	62	14.00	13.75	13.93
28	7.20	6.95	7.13	63	14.20	13.95	14.13
29	7.40	7.15	7.33	64	14.40	14.15	14.33
30	7.60	7.35	7.53	65	14.60	14.35	14.53
31	7.80	7.55	7.73	66	14.80	14.55	14.73
32	8.00	7.75	7.93	67	15.00	14.75	14.93
33	8.20	7.95	8.13	68	15.20	14.95	15.13
34	8.40	8.15	8.33	69	15.40	15.15	15.33
35	8.60	8.35	8.53	70	15.60	15.35	15.53

Exhibit 711.32 Special Fourth-Class Rates
Note: Compute postage at the above rates for each addressed piece.

Library Rate

Weight Not Exceeding (Lbs.)	Single Piece Rate	Weight Not Exceeding (Lbs.)	Single Piece Rate	Weight Not Exceeding (Pounds)	Single Piece Rate
1	$.64	24	$4.06	47	$6.82
2	.87	25	4.18	48	6.94
3	1.10	26	4.30	49	7.06
4	1.33	27	4.42	50	7.18
5	1.56	28	4.54	51	7.30
6	1.79	29	4.66	52	7.42
7	2.02	30	4.78	53	7.54
8	2.14	31	4.90	54	7.66
9	2.26	32	5.02	55	7.78
10	2.38	33	5.14	56	7.90
11	2.50	34	5.26	57	8.02
12	2.62	35	5.38	58	8.14
13	2.74	36	5.50	59	8.26
14	2.86	37	5.62	60	8.38
15	2.98	38	5.74	61	8.50
16	3.10	39	5.86	62	8.62
17	3.22	40	5.98	63	8.74
18	3.34	41	6.10	64	8.86
19	3.46	42	6.22	65	8.98
20	3.58	43	6.34	66	9.10
21	3.70	44	6.46	67	9.22
22	3.82	45	6.58	68	9.34
23	3.94	46	6.70	69	9.46
				70	9.58

Exhibit 711.42-Library Rate
Note: Compute postage at the above rates for each addressed piece.

www.ingramcontent.com/pod-product-compliance
Lightning Source LLC
Chambersburg PA
CBHW082125230426
43671CB00015B/2814